T0024549

THE LITTLE RED BOOK

STUDY GUIDE

About the Author

Bill P. has worked in the alcohol and drug addiction field for eighteen years as counselor, historian, educator, and author. He completed his master's degree in addiction studies with an internship at the Alcoholics Anonymous Headquarters archives. He also worked four years on the *A.A. Grapevine* magazine.

While researching the background of the *Little Red Book*'s fiftieth anniversary edition, important new information was found regarding the authors Ed Webster and Barry Collins. As the popularity of the book increased in the 1950s, various study guide formats were put together across Canada and New England. The Step study guides have been called the Novalco Method and AAWOL (An Alcoholic's Way of Life).

Bill P. has taken the information from Ed Webster's notes and the many past formats and compiled and written this new study guide to the time-honored classic, *The Little Red Book*.

About the Book

This study guide for *The Little Red Book* is designed to meet both the needs of AA study groups and those of newcomers to AA who are working the program on their own. Long regarded as *the* guide to the Twelve Steps, *The Little Red Book* draws from the practical experience of alcoholics who found peace of mind and sobriety through Alcoholics Anonymous. Modeled after Twelve Step instruction programs offered at AA meetings, this new guide provides a solid and comprehensive tool for studying *The Little Red Book*. While *The Little Red Book* interprets the Twelve Steps, *The Little Red Book Study Guide* gives newcomers to AA the structure needed to live them.

About Hazelden Publishing

As part of the Hazelden Betty Ford Foundation, Hazelden Publishing offers both cutting-edge educational resources and inspirational books. Our print and digital works help guide individuals in treatment and recovery, and their loved ones. Professionals who work to prevent and treat addiction also turn to Hazelden Publishing for evidence-based curricula, digital content solutions, and videos for use in schools, treatment programs, correctional programs, and electronic health records systems. We also offer training for implementation of our curricula.

Through published and digital works, Hazelden Publishing extends the reach of healing and hope to individuals, families, and communities affected by addiction and related issues.

For more information about Hazelden publications, please call **800-328-9000** or visit us online at **hazelden.org/bookstore**.

THE LITTLE
RED BOOK

STUDY GUIDE

BILL P.

Hazelden
Publishing

Hazelden Publishing
www.hazelden.org/bookstore

©1998 by Hazelden Foundation
All rights reserved
Printed in the United States of America
No portion of this publication may be reproduced
in any manner without the written permission
of the publisher, except the Daily Inventory Log,
My Daily Inventory, and My Daily Inventory Review—
all of which are reproducible for personal use.

ISBN: 1-56838-283-9

Book design and typesetting by Evans McCormick Creative
Cover design by David Spohn

Editor's note:

The Twelve Steps and Twelve Traditions are reprinted with permission of Alcoholics Anonymous World Services, Inc. Permission to reprint the Twelve Steps and Twelve Traditions does not mean that AA has reviewed or approved the contents of this publication, nor that AA agrees with the views expressed herein. AA is a program of recovery from alcoholism *only*—use of the Twelve Steps and Twelve Traditions in connection with programs and activities which are patterned after AA, but which address other problems, or in any other non-AA context, does not imply otherwise.

To the memory of
Barry Collins
and
Ed Webster

The answers will come,
If your own house is in order.

—ALCOHOLICS ANONYMOUS
PAGE 164

Contents

CONTENTS CONTINUED

 **INTRODUCTION**

HOW TO USE THIS BOOK

The following guide is to be used with the 1986 revised hardcover edition or the paperback edition of *The Little Red Book,* both of which are available from Hazelden. (This study guide does not correspond to the page numbers in the 50th Anniversary edition of *The Little Red Book.*) When paragraphs numbers are shown in this guide, count down from the first full paragraph on the page indicated in *The Little Red Book.*

This guide lists key ideas from *The Little Red Book.* Most study groups and individuals highlight or underline the key ideas in their *Little Red Book* and write the corresponding key idea numbers in the margin. This method helps as a chairperson may refer to a certain key idea during discussion periods.

Groups and individuals can set up various formats for using this study guide. One popular method is to use the study guide during twenty-four weekly meetings. Chairpersons may easily adapt this study guide to any length for group study, and individuals may choose their pace.

Most groups using the guide sit in a circle so everyone can see each other. The chairperson opens the meeting and conducts whatever preliminaries are chosen by the group: having a moment of silence, reciting the Serenity Prayer, doing roll call, or collecting donations. Most groups read a chapter from *The Little Red Book,* taking turns with each paragraph or page. After a key idea is read, the chairperson stops and begins the group discussion. At the end of the week's study, the chairperson assigns homework for the next meeting and asks for a renewed commitment from each member to finish the selected sessions from the study guide.

Whether you are a newcomer or have been in the program for many years, a study of the Twelve Steps in sequence is a time-honored tradition that can only be helpful.

 **LESSON ONE**

THE PROGRAM OF ALCOHOLICS ANONYMOUS

KEY IDEA 1

We too often fail to realize the extent to which we are physically, mentally, and spiritually ill.

HARDCOVER*	PAPERBACK
PAGE 5, PARAGRAPH 4	PAGE 5, PARAGRAPH 4

SUGGESTION FOR SELF-STUDY OR GROUP DISCUSSION

Give personal examples of how the disease demonstrated itself in our lives in this threefold manner. Although we have come to the Alcoholics Anonymous program to stop our addiction, what we will find is a way to start living.

KEY IDEA 2

Recovery through the AA program is simple.

HARDCOVER	PAPERBACK
PAGE 6, PARAGRAPH 1	PAGE 6, PARAGRAPH 2

SUGGESTION FOR SELF-STUDY OR GROUP DISCUSSION

Recovery is a way of life, not a course of study—otherwise all we would have to do is learn the Big Book and we would be cured. We are often reminded to remember the slogan, *Keep It Simple Stupid*, or KISS. As we are what we think, all that we are comes from our thoughts and with our thoughts we make the world.

---

*Shaded regions are a reference guide to *The Little Red Book*.

KEY IDEA 3

AA is not a religion.

HARDCOVER	PAPERBACK
PAGE 6, PARAGRAPH 2	PAGE 6, PARAGRAPH 3

SUGGESTION FOR SELF-STUDY OR GROUP DISCUSSION

The purpose of any religion is to foster spirituality among its followers. Religion is not the only source of spirituality. Religion demands specific behavior; spirituality is a positive and creative attitude about life. We hear some members say, "Religion is for people who don't want to go to hell, spirituality is for those who have been there." AA has nothing against organized religion. It even suggests that members consider returning to the religion of their childhood.

KEY IDEA 4

Stringent honesty is an absolute requirement of rehabilitation.

HARDCOVER	PAPERBACK
PAGE 6, PARAGRAPH 4	PAGE 6, BOTTOM
	PAGE 7, TOP

SUGGESTION FOR SELF-STUDY OR GROUP DISCUSSION

Alcoholism is a disease of denial. We often use rationalization to justify unacceptable behavior. At the end of each day, we review our actions and ask ourselves if we have been honest in all we have said and done. Honesty in recovery takes practice, so we practice as if our lives depend on it. They do!

KEY IDEA 5

But plain sobriety is not enough.

HARDCOVER	PAPERBACK
PAGE 7, PARAGRAPH 2	PAGE 7, PARAGRAPH 3

SUGGESTION FOR SELF-STUDY OR GROUP DISCUSSION

There is a difference between being dry and being sober. Those who are dry aren't willing to learn or change. Those who are sober are willing to learn the simple facts of their threefold illness and practice the principles and Steps of the program. This leads to wisdom and lasting, contented recovery.

KEY IDEA 6

We must acquire honesty, humility, and appreciation, and kill self-centeredness to keep sober.

HARDCOVER	PAPERBACK
PAGE 7, PARAGRAPH 2	PAGE 7, PARAGRAPH 3

SUGGESTION FOR SELF-STUDY OR GROUP DISCUSSION

The way to accomplish this is by doing the Steps, particularly in sequence. Selfishness and self-centeredness are created by too much concern for who we are and what we will be. Self-centeredness leads to a complete failure in working the program. We are encouraged in recovery to become "other-centered," thus getting our minds off ourselves.

Key Idea 7

We recommend a close study of the book *Alcoholics Anonymous*.

Hardcover	Paperback
Page 7, Paragraph 3	Page 7, Paragraph 4

Suggestion for self-study or group discussion

The Big Book is the foundation of the entire program. How many have read the Big Book cover to cover?

Key Idea 8

We merely strive toward perfecting ourselves.

Hardcover	Paperback
Page 8, Paragraph 2	Page 8, Paragraph 2

Suggestion for self-study or group discussion

We will only achieve perfection once we are dead. Therefore the goal is not in the accomplishment but in the process. The secret is to find joy in the effort. We often hear, "Recovery is a journey, not a destination." We give up trying to be perfect and control everything. We work at being human, "not-god" as our active addictive behavior led us to believe. We remember that the program tells us: "We are not saints. Progress, not perfection."

KEY IDEA 9

Humility: A true evaluation of conditions as they are.

HARDCOVER	PAPERBACK
PAGE 8, PARAGRAPH 4	PAGE 9, PARAGRAPH 1

SUGGESTION FOR SELF-STUDY OR GROUP DISCUSSION

Humility is essential to our spiritual progress, and our spiritual progress is a necessary part of recovery. Humility is my acceptance of myself.

KEY IDEA 10

Honesty: Freedom from self-deception.

HARDCOVER	PAPERBACK
PAGE 9, PARAGRAPH 1	PAGE 9, PARAGRAPH 2

SUGGESTION FOR SELF-STUDY OR GROUP DISCUSSION

We examine every thought and action to make sure it's right or wrong for us. If we don't feel good about it, we correct it as soon as it becomes clear to us that we've made a mistake. Learning to trust our thoughts and feelings takes time and practice.

KEY IDEA 11

Faith: Reliance, hope, and trust in the AA program.

HARDCOVER	PAPERBACK
PAGE 9, PARAGRAPH 2	PAGE 9, PARAGRAPH 3

SUGGESTION FOR SELF-STUDY OR GROUP DISCUSSION

Blind faith in our Twelve Step program was all that many of us had to our credit when we began recovery. Today we realize it is one of the most important assets in the search for spiritual progress. With the acceptance of our program's living principles comes the gift of belief that we can change fear into faith.

KEY IDEA 12

Courage: A quality of mind which enables us to deal with the problems and realities of life without reliance on alcohol.

HARDCOVER	PAPERBACK
PAGE 9, PARAGRAPH 3	PAGE 9, PARAGRAPH 4

SUGGESTION FOR SELF-STUDY OR GROUP DISCUSSION

Courage is what makes us do the right thing even when nobody else is doing it. We can find happiness while surrounded by darkness. We can be loving in the middle of hate and envy. We can be serene when surrounded by chaos, fear, and anger. "Let truth and faith give me courage, so that when fear knocks, no one is there."

KEY IDEA 13

Gratitude: Gratitude continues the miracle of our sobriety.

HARDCOVER	PAPERBACK
PAGE 9, PARAGRAPH 4	PAGE 10, PARAGRAPH 1

SUGGESTION FOR SELF-STUDY OR GROUP DISCUSSION

There are many adjustments to be made in our recovery. We are careful how we judge our progress. The program provides us with a new pair of glasses to see our new world. Those glasses are uncomfortable to us at first. We slowly learn in recovery to count our blessings and work toward an "attitude of gratitude."

KEY IDEA 14

Service: Service to God and our fellow human beings is the key to AA success.

HARDCOVER	PAPERBACK
PAGE 10, PARAGRAPH 1	PAGE 10, PARAGRAPH 2

SUGGESTION FOR SELF-STUDY OR GROUP DISCUSSION

One of the Three Legacies of our Fellowship is *service* along with *unity* and *recovery*. No effort must seem so great that it will stop us from giving completely of ourselves in helping someone find the kind of life others are helping us find. We learn that in the act of one person helping another, no person can give without receiving, or get without giving.

 **LESSON TWO**

STEP ONE

*We admitted we were powerless over alcohol—that our lives
had become unmanageable.*

No one likes to admit complete defeat, and this first Step on the road
to recovery makes all of our natural instincts cry out against accepting this
idea. We think we are able to control every aspect of our lives, but this one
thing—our drinking—cannot be controlled.

No other kind of bankruptcy is like this one. Alcohol bleeds us of all
our self-sufficiency and the will to resist its demands. We seem to survive
in most other matters, but in this one area we've become helpless. The
way we drank was self-destructive, and we have become used to sabotag-
ing our lives and those around us.

When we enter AA we take another view of this defeat. Through this
defeat we become victorious. Through this humiliation we can find
strength. *The more we can admit defeat the more firm will be our bedrock upon
which we can build a happy and purposeful life.*

Little good can come to us in joining forces with AA, unless we admit
this in the beginning. In this admission of complete defeat we will find
enduring strength. If we do not admit this defeat we will keep trying to
control our drinking, and we will get deeper and deeper into trouble.

We have given up the idea of controlling our drinking because we have
tried it and failed. We also know that willpower alone is futile. If this were
possible we would have licked it already. *It is a statistical fact that alcoholics
rarely stop drinking alone, and those who do are dry by endurance and are
unhappy people. These are difficult people to be around.*

During the early days of AA only the most hopeless grasped this idea of defeat and were saved. Many less desperate could not make this admission of hopelessness. Today many are able to make this admission before they go way down to the bottom. The face of AA has changed, and many are spared these years of hell by making this admission early. From the experience of others we know where we will end up if we drink again. Addiction to alcohol and other drugs is a fatal progressive illness. We can reverse this process, however, by embracing this first Step, as completely as we are able at this time.

Few people will really try AA until they are hurt. AA teaches us things that are hard, and we always look for the easy way out.

After admitting that we are no longer in control, then we must accept this fact. That is just as hard. Webster's dictionary says "acceptance is to receive with consent." So it is with alcoholism. If we agree to live by AA's suggested program, we do not drink. We shall live with alcoholism rather than die from it.

KEY IDEA 1

Recovery is possible for alcoholics who honestly want to stop drinking.

HARDCOVER	PAPERBACK
PAGE 14, PARAGRAPH 4	PAGE 14, PARAGRAPH 4

SUGGESTION FOR SELF-STUDY OR GROUP DISCUSSION

Willingness is all that is needed. A good test for willingness is to answer honestly, *To what lengths am I willing to go to achieve sobriety?* To be willing is to be ready and prepared. We can always profit by being strong-willed, as long as that means "strong-willingness," not hardheadedness.

KEY IDEA 2

In twelve simple Steps they outlined a way of life for daily practice that restored them to physical health and contented sobriety.

HARDCOVER	PAPERBACK
PAGE 14, PARAGRAPH 5	PAGE 15, TOP

SUGGESTION FOR SELF-STUDY OR GROUP DISCUSSION

A difference exists between *program* and *fellowship*. Program is the Twelve Steps and Twelve Traditions. Fellowship is the support and example we give and receive. Countless troubled people have agonized and sometimes died, many by their own hand, because they had given up hope. They never learned that they needed help in solving what seemed like overwhelming problems. It's not a sign of weakness to ask for help. It's a sign of strength.

KEY IDEA 3

A marked personality change, influenced chiefly by negative thinking, now drives the alcoholic to heavier drinking.

HARDCOVER	PAPERBACK
PAGE 17, BOTTOM	PAGE 18, PARAGRAPH 1
PAGE 18, TOP	

SUGGESTION FOR SELF-STUDY OR GROUP DISCUSSION

Beware of rationalizing by blaming people, places, and things or soothing guilt with self-pity and the "if onlys": "If only people understood me." "If only I had a job." We often hear that the alcoholic is the last one to find out that he or she is an alcoholic. Everyone around this person knows the alcoholic needs help.

KEY IDEA 4

There is no shortcut, no substitute, no other way out for the alcoholic.

HARDCOVER	PAPERBACK
PAGE 18, PARAGRAPH 2	PAGE 18, PARAGRAPH 3

SUGGESTION FOR SELF-STUDY OR GROUP DISCUSSION

Referring to acceptance, the Big Book says, "Halfway measures availed us nothing." What does "fake it 'til you make it" mean? AA is for "real alcoholics" who will stop drinking someday. It's always better they are alive when it happens.

KEY IDEA 5

The alcoholic's future security depends on the successful attainment of AA as a way of life.

HARDCOVER	PAPERBACK
PAGE 19, PARAGRAPH 3	PAGE 19, PARAGRAPH 5

SUGGESTION FOR SELF-STUDY OR GROUP DISCUSSION

Functioning in an alcohol-free lifestyle is possible, even though we fear that we or this lifestyle will be boring. Boredom is a form of conceit. When we are bored we are saying, *Okay, life, you are not doing your job of keeping me entertained.* This thinking can poison our attitude and take us back to the point where our addiction seems like the only way out of that boredom.

KEY IDEA 6

Reflect upon your powerlessness over this sickness.

HARDCOVER	PAPERBACK
PAGE 19, PARAGRAPH 5	PAGE 20, PARAGRAPH 2

SUGGESTION FOR SELF-STUDY OR GROUP DISCUSSION

Insanity is taking that first drink, each time expecting different results. Living in that world of being out of control was strange and crazy. Everything was turned around: Right was left, up was down, good was bad, and day was night.

KEY IDEA 7

Consider your inability to take it or leave it alone.

HARDCOVER	PAPERBACK
PAGE 20, TOP	PAGE 20, PARAGRAPH 2

SUGGESTION FOR SELF-STUDY OR GROUP DISCUSSION

Look at examples of promises and firm resolve repeatedly broken. We all have one more slip in us, but do we have one more recovery? We need to always "remember when." When we forget about our First Step, we are setting ourselves up to drink again.

KEY IDEA 8

There is no mystery about it.

HARDCOVER	PAPERBACK
PAGE 20, PARAGRAPH 2	PAGE 21, PARAGRAPH 1

SUGGESTION FOR SELF-STUDY OR GROUP DISCUSSION

The Steps are the only proven way. Pride tells me that I am different, that I can do it my way.

 **LESSON THREE**

STEP TWO

Came to believe that a Power greater than ourselves could restore us to sanity.

When we enter AA, we are told that we must surrender completely to the fact that by ourselves we can do nothing to control our lives, in regard to drinking. This is often humiliating. In Step Two the humiliation goes further. We are told that we must surrender to a Higher Power to get help. This is extremely hard for two reasons. First, it's hard for us to give up our sick ego. Second, this business of a Higher Power brings up the idea of a God, and many of us won't or can't believe in God. Where do we go from there?

Some of us might confuse our talk about God or a Higher Power with religion. Let us clear this up. We never talk religion in AA, although those who fully embrace AA will sometimes seek out or return to a religion they feel comfortable with. We *do* talk about spiritual values. The difference between religion and spiritual values is most evident. Religion is belonging to a certain organized society that believes in a set number of doctrines with specific obligations to fulfill. Spirituality is something personal: one's own set of nonmaterialistic values. A person can be religious but not spiritual or vice versa.

Let us look at the words in Step Two.

Came…The first word means a slow process. It does not have to happen all at once. When we drink the first things that go are our spiritual values. They have to. Otherwise, we would have to stop drinking. When we get to AA we are spiritually bankrupt.

When we stop drinking it is our spiritual values that will be the last to return. Our physical condition improves first. Then our mental condition improves. Finally, our spiritual values return. We came—we came to—we came to believe.

   *…to believe…*This brings up the question of faith or belief in God or a Higher Power. Everyone who enters AA can find himself or herself in one of three groups:

1. THERE ARE THOSE WHO WON'T BELIEVE IN A HIGHER POWER. These usually are the belligerent types. They are their own source of power. Their sobriety is no more than a never-ending painful endurance test. We respect their opinion and ask them to respect ours also. We are not about to enter into theological debate about the existence of God since everyone has his or her own concept of a Higher Power. All AA suggests to these people is that our experience shows there is an easier and less painful way of doing it.

2. THERE ARE THOSE WHO ONCE HAD FAITH IN GOD, BUT FOR SOME REASON OR OTHER THEY HAVE LOST IT. By far most people are in this group. They may have had religion forced on them in their youth and now rebel against it. There are many that have had personal tragedy in their lives and conclude that belief in God is useless. There are those who asked God for help with their drinking but received no response, thus abandoning God. These people usually become indifferent toward God or bitter. They want things their way and would only accept solutions when they could see them. Closed minds cannot see alternatives. When unreasonable demands were not met they began to pout.

3. Finally, there are those who still believe in God, believe they are faithful in their religious practices, but are still having trouble.

God does not seem to help them. They are good churchgoers. They pray, take pledges, and so on—but to no avail. Here the quality of faith should be examined rather than the quantity of religious practices. A superficial, emotional, or romantic approach to faith is of little value.

> *...sanity...*Sanity means *soundness of mind.* Insanity, not mental illness, is to repeat the same behavior over and over, each time expecting a different result. This was our pattern of drinking, the reasoning behind all those broken promises, not even noticing as our lives fell apart around us. We lost contact with reality so slowly we didn't notice it.

> The purpose of this Step—to re-examine our faith—is humility. To be humble is to be teachable. As old-timers in the program often say, "We never stop learning. We will always be a student in our program. We remain teachable. We continue to open our minds to accept and our hearts to understand."

KEY IDEA 1

Wherever alcohol has been involved, we have been strangely insane.

HARDCOVER	PAPERBACK
Page 23, Paragraph 1	Page 23, Paragraph 1

SUGGESTION FOR SELF-STUDY OR GROUP DISCUSSION

We define *sanity* as soundness of mind. Give examples of believing, from your experience, that insanity is doing the same thing over and over each time, expecting a different result.

KEY IDEA 2

Dodging the truth only results in distorted thinking and opposition to help from a Power greater than ourselves.

HARDCOVER	PAPERBACK
PAGE 23, PARAGRAPH 2	PAGE 23, PARAGRAPH 2

SUGGESTION FOR SELF-STUDY OR GROUP DISCUSSION

Having an "open mind" is not being defensive or having reservations. One of our most often used slogans is HOW—Honesty, Open-mindedness, Willingness.

KEY IDEA 3

Our sick personalities find a sure source of power and healing in *God, as we understand Him*.

HARDCOVER	PAPERBACK
PAGE 23, BOTTOM	PAGE 24, PARAGRAPH 1
PAGE 24, TOP	

SUGGESTION FOR SELF-STUDY OR GROUP DISCUSSION

We no longer feel threatened. We are less trapped by grandiosity and perfectionism. This allows us to be human and learn from our mistakes. We are no longer so victimized that we have to be right all the time. We repeat a simple prayer, "Accept me as I am, so that I may learn what I can become."

KEY IDEA 4

The important thing is that we believe in It.

HARDCOVER	PAPERBACK
PAGE 24, PARAGRAPH 1	PAGE 24, PARAGRAPH 2

SUGGESTION FOR SELF-STUDY OR GROUP DISCUSSION

What we choose as a Higher Power is not important as long as we believe that It can help us. One of the basic reasons why we are told to believe in a Power greater than ourselves is so we stop trying to play God.

KEY IDEA 5

Faith in a Higher Power is a basic law of recovery.

HARDCOVER	PAPERBACK
PAGE 24, PARAGRAPH 2	PAGE 24, PARAGRAPH 3

SUGGESTION FOR SELF-STUDY OR GROUP DISCUSSION

When something of value is taken from us we need something of equal or greater value to take its place. Faith is a good replacement for FEAR—Frustration, Ego, Anxiety, and Resentment.

KEY IDEA 6

Use of the word *sanity* offends our false pride.

HARDCOVER	PAPERBACK
PAGE 24, PARAGRAPH 3	PAGE 24, PARAGRAPH 4

SUGGESTION FOR SELF-STUDY OR GROUP DISCUSSION

Alcohol enabled us to lead false lives. We now have to admit that we were phonies. Our acceptance of our alcoholism is not passive but based in reality and truth.

KEY IDEA 7

It might be suicidal to disagree with any part of it, so resolve to be open-minded and accept the Twelve Steps in their entirety.

HARDCOVER	PAPERBACK
PAGE 25, TOP	PAGE 25, TOP

SUGGESTION FOR SELF-STUDY OR GROUP DISCUSSION

Do I have another chance at recovery or will another drinking bout find me dead? Open-mindedness will prevent selfishness and reduce the possibility of painful resentments by not allowing us to be intolerant or form prejudices.

KEY IDEA 8

We believe and know from experience that a Power greater than ourselves can remove this obsession, straighten the twisted thinking, and restore the alcoholic to sane thought and behavior.

HARDCOVER	PAPERBACK
PAGE 27, PARAGRAPH 1	PAGE 27, PARAGRAPH 2

SUGGESTION FOR SELF-STUDY OR GROUP DISCUSSION

Our way didn't work. We have proof from the people who have gone before us that the program does work. There is something bigger than ourselves that we must believe in and trust completely for our sanity, peace of mind, and happiness.

KEY IDEA 9

This encourages deception over our real mental health and fitness; it breeds a superior feeling of false security.

HARDCOVER	PAPERBACK
PAGE 27, PARAGRAPH 4	PAGE 27, PARAGRAPH 5

SUGGESTION FOR SELF-STUDY OR GROUP DISCUSSION

To drink the way we did, we had to rationalize and justify what we were doing. The only way to do this was to distort reality. We thought our journeys outside reality brought us peace and serenity. When we returned to reality we found harshness and pain. So it went, day after day, week after week, month after month, year after year. Run, escape, pain. Run, escape, pain.

KEY IDEA 10

Sobriety, sanity, security, and peace of mind are within our reach.

HARDCOVER	PAPERBACK
PAGE 29, BOTTOM	PAGE 30, TOP
PAGE 30, TOP	

SUGGESTION FOR SELF-STUDY OR GROUP DISCUSSION

Our alcoholism wouldn't let us escape anymore, even when we tried using more heavily. All that was left of our lives was pain and insanity. Our program shows us that reality isn't a problem, but trying to escape reality is.

KEY IDEA 11

In spite of all knowledge, some of us willfully continue in self-centeredness.

HARDCOVER	PAPERBACK
PAGE 30, PARAGRAPH 3	PAGE 30, PARAGRAPH 3

SUGGESTION FOR SELF-STUDY OR GROUP DISCUSSION

Rather than relate our feelings to the outside world, we make the outside world fit our feelings. This is a program to be lived. This is a program of positive action. We trust and believe that the changes asked of us are necessary and good for us.

 **LESSON FOUR**

STEP THREE

Made a decision to turn our will and our lives over to the
care of God as we understood Him.

The practice of Step Three is like opening a door to a new life. All we have to do is make the decision and it is ours. The key to the door is willingness. Effort in this Step yields great rewards.

The first two Steps call for acceptance. The Third Step requires positive action in order to accomplish it. This is the first of the *action* Steps. With the successful completion of this Step, an individual can remain sober by virtue of a Higher Power rather than by virtue of endurance.

Let us look at the words in Step Three.

Made refers to positive action. In our drinking days we took very self-destructive actions. Now we take action to reverse this course and seek help from someone or something greater than ourselves in order to lead more fruitful and happy lives.

Decision is from Latin and it means to cut in half. When we make a decision about a problem, we cut it in half. When we decide to let a Higher Power help us with our drinking, we have half solved our problem.

We see it works for other people; therefore, it can work for us. All we are asked is to try to make a beginning. Even the smallest beginning is all that is needed. The great enemy of this Step is delaying this decision.

The mere fact that we are here indicates that we want to do something about our drinking. In other words, we have made some decisions.

To turn my will and my life over is a matter of trust that usually involves trial and error. We wonder, *Do I lose my identity? Do I become the hole in the doughnut? Or does it mean enjoying the fruit of someone else's work so that I might attain my true destiny? In my tunnel vision I cannot perceive what my true nature is.*

We have always functioned in the delusion that we were controlling our own lives. We had a false sense of security. Even though we now see that our way didn't work, we still feel threatened by the request to risk a Higher Power doing it for us.

KEY IDEA 1

Our great need is loss of self-centeredness and alcoholic obsession.

HARDCOVER	PAPERBACK
PAGE 34, PARAGRAPH 1	PAGE 34, PARAGRAPH 3

SUGGESTION FOR SELF-STUDY OR GROUP DISCUSSION

Wisdom is the ability to perceive alternatives. In our alcoholic thinking we insisted that only we knew what was good for us. When we decide to turn our will and lives over we make a declaration of independence. We declare our freedom from the chains of our self-centered ego and the unrelenting demands of self-will. When we decide that God is god and we are not, we begin to receive the wonderful future that has been planned for us.

KEY IDEA 2

When we have made this crucial decision, our attitude changes rapidly from negative to wholesome, constructive thinking.

HARDCOVER	PAPERBACK
PAGE 34, PARAGRAPH 3	PAGE 34, BOTTOM
	PAGE 35, TOP

SUGGESTION FOR SELF-STUDY OR GROUP DISCUSSION

Alcoholic thinking is muddled and defensive, constantly rationalizing for justification. The need for others in recovery and a sponsor as objective references is evident. We find reality never changes, but our attitude toward it can. How we react to reality makes our reality.

KEY IDEA 3

We are advised the AA program is simple.

HARDCOVER	PAPERBACK
PAGE 36, PARAGRAPH 2	PAGE 36, PARAGRAPH 2

SUGGESTION FOR SELF-STUDY OR GROUP DISCUSSION

Utilize don't analyze. Identify don't compare. The emphasis here is on doing. Understanding will come later. Intellectualizing can be a stall tactic, a cop out. When we're always in our own heads, we're behind enemy lines.

KEY IDEA 4

We should not confuse organized religion with AA.

HARDCOVER	PAPERBACK
PAGE 37, PARAGRAPH 1	PAGE 37, PARAGRAPH 2

SUGGESTION FOR SELF-STUDY OR GROUP DISCUSSION

Who or what have we chosen for our Higher Power? It is helpful at this time to decide on our own Higher Power rather than assume one that has been defined for us.

KEY IDEA 5

Since this is no overnight process, we suggest thought and prayer in the matter.

HARDCOVER	PAPERBACK
PAGE 37, PARAGRAPH 4	PAGE 38, PARAGRAPH 1

SUGGESTION FOR SELF-STUDY OR GROUP DISCUSSION

Most people experience a slow process of "spiritual awakening," even though a few, such as Bill W. in his story in the Big Book, experience a sudden and dramatic one. Sometimes spiritual progress may seem slow to us, but if we honestly work the program, that progress is sure.

KEY IDEA 6

We demand maturity without the pains of experience and growth.

HARDCOVER	PAPERBACK
PAGE 38, PARAGRAPH 4	PAGE 39, PARAGRAPH 1

SUGGESTION FOR SELF-STUDY OR GROUP DISCUSSION

Maturity is the ability to postpone immediate gratification. Emotionally immature, we want what we want, when we want it. When we act like babies, we think we are the center of the universe. When we admit defeat, we need to put our childish behavior behind us. We change from believing in Baby Power to believing in a Higher Power.

KEY IDEA 7

Procrastination and skepticism are enemies of spiritual attainment.

HARDCOVER	PAPERBACK
PAGE 39, PARAGRAPH 1	PAGE 39, PARAGRAPH 2

SUGGESTION FOR SELF-STUDY OR GROUP DISCUSSION

Alcoholics are romantic dreamers. They want life to happen to them rather than take the initiative to participate in life. An American proverb reminds us, "Success is a ladder that cannot be climbed with your hands in your pockets."

KEY IDEA 8

We stop playing God. We surrender our self-centeredness to Him.

HARDCOVER	PAPERBACK
PAGE 44, PARAGRAPH 3	PAGE 44, PARAGRAPH 5

SUGGESTION FOR SELF-STUDY OR GROUP DISCUSSION

Humility enables us to surrender to win. Our decision in the Third Step is our claim to a new way of life. The prison of our sick egos that was our home is slowly being destroyed. We decide to Let Go and Let God daily.

 **Lesson Five**

Step Four

Made a searching and fearless moral inventory of ourselves.

Step Four is an action Step. This Step grates on the alcoholic nature. We begin the process of reversing many of the survival behaviors necessary to sustain an active alcoholic. We do not enjoy these self-destructive behaviors, but we have become accustomed to using them.

Made…This Step demands positive action. It is not accomplished all at once, but gradually. There are two theories about taking this Step:

1. Don't take it until you are absolutely ready.

2. Take it right away.

Possibly the combination of these two ideas holds more value. Ease into it, but remember to be gentle on yourself.

Searching and fearless means being as honest as you can be at the moment. We are used to rationalizing, so sincerity is mandatory.

In doing a *moral inventory* we want to take advantage of our assets in order to work on our liabilities. Our behavior indicates attitudes and personalities, but don't get stuck in details. Try to see through the phony behavior.

This is not an examination of conscience. We are not only looking for sins and evil deeds we might have done in the past. We are looking for personality traits and conflicts that cause us distress.

Inventory is from a Latin word that means *to find*. We are looking for character defects and shortcomings that cause us problems.

We are all endowed by nature with certain wonderful and powerful instincts; otherwise, we would not have survived. Our problem is that in our disease we have exercised some of these instincts to the extreme, and it has become a way of life that we now see as destructive. The Steps address these misdirected instincts.

Step Four is a vigorous and painstaking effort to discover what these liabilities in each of us have been and are now. By discovering what our emotional conflicts are, we can move toward their correction. We cannot do this without taking a good look at ourselves.

The alcoholic cannot live with discomfort for great periods of time without eventually seeking relief in alcohol.

There are many ways to take Step Four. Do it in whatever way appeals to you. Make sure it is written down, however. You *must* believe no one will ever read it—not even when you do the Fifth Step. It is the only way we can be completely honest with ourselves.

STEP FOUR

MAKE A SEARCHING AND FEARLESS MORAL INVENTORY FOR OURSELVES

The following pages can guide you as you start on Step Four. On pages 31–32, check what is applicable to yourself. On pages 33–40, you can write specific examples of how some of these positive and negative qualities apply to you. This exercise will help you to continue with your own insights into your feelings and behaviors.

ASSETS	LIABILITIES
❑ Thoughtful of others	❑ Self-pitying
❑ Not holding grudges (forgiving)	❑ Resentful
❑ Charitable	❑ Critical
❑ Trusting	❑ Suspicious
❑ Patient	❑ Impatient
❑ Relaxed	❑ Tense and apprehensive
❑ Calm	❑ Emotionally uncontrolled
❑ Outgoing	❑ Withdrawn
❑ Loving in attitude	❑ Jealous
❑ Confident	❑ Fearful
❑ Generous	❑ Self-indulgent
❑ Yielding	❑ Domineering
❑ Kind	❑ Angry, hateful
❑ Positive in outlook	❑ Obsessed with own problems
❑ Uncritical	❑ Self-righteous
❑ Agreeable	❑ Stubborn
❑ Forgiving	❑ Intolerant
❑ Truthful	❑ Dishonest
❑ Cheerful, optimistic	❑ Gloomy, depressed

Continued on next page

Assets	Liabilities
❑ Gracious, open-minded	❑ Smug, narrow-minded
❑ Humble	❑ Prideful (feeling superior)
❑ Realistic	❑ Unrealistic
❑ Willing to admit faults	❑ Hypersensitive
❑ Hopeful	❑ Despondent
❑ Having a sense of humor	❑ Sullen (silent treatment)
❑ Content	❑ Apprehensive
❑ Being prompt	❑ Procrastinating
❑ Purposeful	❑ Indifferent
❑ Serene	❑ Worrisome
❑ Confidential	❑ Gossiping
❑ Helpful	❑ Self-absorbed
❑ Unselfishness	❑ Self-pitying
❑ Modesty	❑ Self-importance
❑ Moral, ethical	❑ Vulgar, immoral in act and thought
❑ Grateful	❑ Feeling entitled
❑ Using sex for bonding	❑ Using sex for validation

STEP FOUR

POSITIVE QUALITIES GUIDE

The following is a partial list of the virtues one might have. It should be used as a guide only. The Steps ask you to examine your exact nature. Give an example of each quality that applies to you.

Humility:

_____

_____

_____

Modesty:

_____

_____

_____

Honesty with oneself:

_____

_____

_____

Patience:

_____

_____

_____

Love:

_____

_____

_____

Forgiveness:

_____

_____

_____

Simplicity:

_____

_____

_____

Trust:

_____

_____

_____

Generosity:

_____

_____

_____

Productiveness:

_____

_____

_____

Creativity:

_____

_____

_____

Promptness:

_____

_____

_____

Straightforwardness:

_____

_____

_____

Positive thinking:

_____

_____

_____

Thoughtfulness:

_____

_____

_____

Optimistic:

_____

_____

_____

Open-mindedness:

_____

_____

_____

Sense of humor:

_____

_____

_____

Graciousness:

_____

_____

_____

Gratefulness:

_____

_____

_____

Helpfulness:

_____

_____

_____

STEP FOUR

NEGATIVE QUALITIES GUIDE

The following is a partial list of defects one might have. It should be used as a guide only. Write an example after each quality that applies to you.

Resentment:

_____

_____

_____

Dishonesty with oneself:

_____

_____

_____

Criticism:

_____

_____

_____

Self-pity:

_____

_____

_____

Jealousy:

_____

_____

_____

Intolerance:

_____

_____

_____

Fear:

_____

_____

_____

Temper:

_____

_____

_____

Impatience:

_____

_____

_____

Hate:

_____

_____

_____

Envy:

_____

_____

_____

False pride:

_____

_____

_____

Laziness:

_____

_____

_____

Procrastination:

_____

_____

_____

Negative thinking:

_____

_____

_____

Suspiciousness:

_____

_____

_____

Selfishness:

_____

_____

_____

Withdrawing:

_____

_____

_____

Self-righteousness:

_____

_____

_____

Despondency:

_____

_____

_____

Ungratefulness:

_____

_____

_____

Prone to gossip:

_____

_____

_____

KEY IDEA 1

We gauge AA personality by AA maturity.

HARDCOVER	PAPERBACK
PAGE 47, PARAGRAPH 3	PAGE 47, PARAGRAPH 3

SUGGESTION FOR SELF-STUDY OR GROUP DISCUSSION

What behaviors and attitudes do you believe indicate maturity? The rewards we receive from the program are equal to the effort we put into our recovery.

KEY IDEA 2

We wish to know why we have been at war with ourselves.

HARDCOVER	PAPERBACK
PAGE 47, PARAGRAPH 4	PAGE 48, PARAGRAPH 1

SUGGESTION FOR SELF-STUDY OR GROUP DISCUSSION

Alcoholism is a disease of denial. We had to deny and distort reality to justify our drinking. Our inventory reflects the negative character traits of the alcoholic personality.

KEY IDEA 3

Arresting our alcoholism is not possible until we have knowledge of our defects.

HARDCOVER	PAPERBACK
PAGE 48, PARAGRAPH 3	PAGE 48, PARAGRAPH 4

SUGGESTION FOR SELF-STUDY OR GROUP DISCUSSION

Alcoholism is threefold: physical, emotional, and spiritual. We cannot change things until we can assess where we stand in these areas and understand ways to correct them.

KEY IDEA 4

Our program is not in accord with halfway measures or efforts.

HARDCOVER	PAPERBACK
PAGE 49, PARAGRAPH 1	PAGE 49, PARAGRAPH 2

SUGGESTION FOR SELF-STUDY OR GROUP DISCUSSION

We have lived phony lives filled with deception, but the greatest con of all was lying to ourselves. We ended up believing our own lies.

KEY IDEA 5

To be effective, it must be a written inventory.

HARDCOVER	PAPERBACK
PAGE 49, PARAGRAPH 2	PAGE 49, PARAGRAPH 3

SUGGESTION FOR SELF-STUDY OR GROUP DISCUSSION

We need to have concrete evidence. We don't want to play mental games with ourselves. We cannot write honestly unless we first decide that no one is ever going to read this—not even in our Fifth Step.

Note: Read and discuss topics of resentment, dishonesty, criticism, self-pity, jealousy, intolerance, fear, anger, and blind spots.

HARDCOVER	PAPERBACK
PAGES 50–66	PAGES 50–66

 **LESSON SIX**

STEP FIVE

Admitted to God, to ourselves, and to another human being
the exact nature of our wrongs.

Recovery is often described as a program of ego reduction. Step Five begins that process. It is a Step that disciplines the ego. We cannot live alone with the ghosts of yesterday. Our fear and shame try to dissuade us from doing this. Our secrets hold serious danger to any lasting recovery. Our secrets are barriers that separate us from all other human beings. These walls are the ultimate source of loneliness.

Step Five frees us from that terrible sense of isolation. It is the beginning of a new kinship with our Higher Power and people. This Step takes away the heavy burden of guilt we have always lived with. It gives us an opportunity for a healthy life, a life lived with humility. We gain a sense of our true selves, and the phony self is put to rest.

We are careful of overdramatizing or exaggerating our defects. Our opinions of ourselves might not be true. We have lived a lie so long we have often come to believe it ourselves. We need an objective source to find reality.

We need to take some consideration in choosing the right person with whom to take this Step, since we will share facts that everyone should not hear. Some suggestions follow.

1. This person should be experienced and know what AA is all about. If this person is not in AA, he or she should be briefed as to the nature of what you are doing. You should choose someone who will not pass judgment.

2. This person should be trustworthy not to repeat anything you might tell him or her. You should feel comfortable in this confidence.

3. He or she should be a person you can talk to freely and openly.

4. If in AA, this person should have long-term sobriety. You don't want to worry about this person relapsing.

5. This person should be someone you feel has had similar experiences and can give validation.

KEY IDEA 1

Step Five is a preparatory Step to the restitution that we expect to make as we carry out the provisions of Step Nine, where amends are necessary and we make them.

HARDCOVER	PAPERBACK
PAGE 67, PARAGRAPH 4	PAGE 70, PARAGRAPH 1

SUGGESTION FOR SELF-STUDY OR GROUP DISCUSSION

To achieve serenity, we must rid ourselves of the guilt from our past unacceptable behavior. The time we spend right now feeling guilty only uses time that we could spend thanking our Higher Power for the moment we are living now. Gratitude will always make mincemeat out of guilt.

KEY IDEA 2

The humility this Step brings us is necessary to our future welfare.

HARDCOVER	PAPERBACK
PAGE 68, PARAGRAPH 4	PAGE 71, PARAGRAPH 1

To drink the way we did, we could not allow anyone to tell us anything. Deep down we knew they would point out our alcoholism. We thought we were in control and safe in our secret.

KEY IDEA 3

We are unconsciously dominated by our old thoughts.

HARDCOVER	PAPERBACK
PAGE 69, TOP	PAGE 71, PARAGRAPH 3

SUGGESTION FOR SELF-STUDY OR GROUP DISCUSSION

Do the "old tapes of escape"—which are always ready to play—ever leave us?

KEY IDEA 4

For this reason, a clergy member, psychiatrist, counselor, or doctor is our best [resource].

HARDCOVER	PAPERBACK
PAGE 69, PARAGRAPH 1	PAGE 72, TOP

SUGGESTION FOR SELF-STUDY OR GROUP DISCUSSION

It is critical that the recipient understands what the Fifth Step is all about. We are not asking for forgiveness here. We are simply acknowledging and accepting our past.

KEY IDEA 5

If in doubt about when to take Step Five—take it immediately.

HARDCOVER	PAPERBACK
PAGE 70, PARAGRAPH 1	PAGE 72, PARAGRAPH 2

SUGGESTION FOR SELF-STUDY OR GROUP DISCUSSION

There is no wrong way to do this Step. All we have to do is ask ourselves, *Is there anything I am deliberately concealing?*

KEY IDEA 6

The Step is a direct challenge to our sincerity.

HARDCOVER	PAPERBACK
PAGE 71, PARAGRAPH 2	PAGE 73, PARAGRAPH 3

SUGGESTION FOR SELF-STUDY OR GROUP DISCUSSION

This Step is proof of how far we are willing to go to achieve contented sobriety.

KEY IDEA 7

Is our work solid so far?

HARDCOVER	PAPERBACK
PAGE 72, TOP	PAGE 74, PARAGRAPH 1

SUGGESTION FOR SELF-STUDY OR GROUP DISCUSSION

The mutual support felt within the group is important. What are each member's feelings thus far? Does anyone feel that some topic has not been covered?

LESSON SEVEN

STEP SIX AND STEP SEVEN

Step Six: *Were entirely ready to have God remove all these defects of character.*

Step Seven: *Humbly asked Him to remove our shortcomings.*

Anyone who is willing and honestly tries this Step has advanced spiritually. Old-timers have proven that this Step works. Watch them and see their inner peace as serenity takes the place of turmoil and conflict.

Just as the obsession for alcohol is lifted, so are our character defects lifted from us. What is promised is more than just not drinking. What is promised is happy and contented sobriety.

Let us look at two words in Step Six: *entirely ready*. We are willing to go to any length in our recovery quest. Few of us can quickly or easily become ready to aim at perfection. How then can we accept the entire implication of Step Six? This Step is a goal toward which we strive. It is a measuring stick by which we can determine our progress. The urgent thing is that we at least make a beginning.

We all have natural drives and instincts. When these drives, instincts, or desires surpass their intended purposes, they then become character defects. When we use them to demand more satisfaction than they are able to deliver, we are left in a disquieting emotional state.

We become successful in attaining a healthy attitude in the trying rather than in the conquest. Step Six is the adoption of an attitude by which we begin a lifetime job of building a better character.

Certain attitudes can be deadly in our quest for recovery. Some of these attitudes are listed at the top of the next page.

- *No Never*   To this Step is a closed mind
- *Delay*   To this Step is dangerous
- *Rebellion*   To this Step is fatal

KEY IDEA 1

The *Spiritual Lift*, the nearness to our Creator that is experienced from humble invocation of His help, and our willingness to be freed from old willful thoughts and habits are essential to successful attainment of these Steps.

HARDCOVER	PAPERBACK
PAGE 73, BOTTOM	PAGE 76, PARAGRAPH 1
PAGE 74, TOP	

SUGGESTION FOR SELF-STUDY OR GROUP DISCUSSION

The ability to take risks is a sign of recovery. This involves not only courage but also trust and self-esteem.

KEY IDEA 2

[We experience] a reconciliation to God's way of doing business. We become "fed up" with our way and with further practice of trying to run the show ourselves.

HARDCOVER	PAPERBACK
PAGE 74, PARAGRAPH 3	PAGE 77, PARAGRAPH 1

SUGGESTION FOR SELF-STUDY OR GROUP DISCUSSION

The imprisonment of *tunnel vision* is broken by the practice of gratitude.

Now we'll look at Step Seven: *Humbly asked Him to remove our shortcomings*. The important point in this Step is humility. In order to sober up there must be some traumatic event that is so shocking and painful (hitting bottom) that it results in a major deflation of egotism. If at this point the alcoholic chooses humility instead of a restoration of false pride and seeks and finds help, the alcoholic has begun his or her journey in recovery.

It is important not to confuse humility with humiliation. Nor is putting oneself down or not owning up to one's attributes humility. That is, in fact, false pride. Humility means having an honest and true picture of ourselves—the positive as well as the negative. Humility means to be *teachable*—we don't have all the answers and it's not true that only we know what is good for us. Humility is to be open. Wisdom is the ability to perceive alternatives.

This Step places character building and spiritual values first. This becomes the main purpose of our lives.

KEY IDEA 3

Knowledge of our illness, alcoholism, prompts us to turn to God for help. The alcoholic must pray. There is no standard form of prayer to use. Our remorse over past mistakes and a genuine desire to correct them will indicate how we shall pray.

HARDCOVER	PAPERBACK
PAGE 75, BOTTOM	PAGE 78, PARAGRAPH 2
PAGE 76, TOP	

SUGGESTION FOR SELF-STUDY OR GROUP DISCUSSION

Spontaneous and creative conversation with our Higher Power produces a more intimate and fruitful relationship.

KEY IDEA 4

We ask for spiritual and physical strength to execute His will.

HARDCOVER	PAPERBACK
PAGE 76, PARAGRAPH 1	PAGE 78, PARAGRAPH 3

SUGGESTION FOR SELF-STUDY OR GROUP DISCUSSION

The "twenty-four-hour" idea is often difficult for the alcoholic to get a handle on. We know God's will if we can stay in the moment.

KEY IDEA 5

We ask God's help; we thank Him for recovery; and we maintain our contented sobriety.

HARDCOVER	PAPERBACK
PAGE 76, PARAGRAPH 2	PAGE 78, PARAGRAPH 4

SUGGESTION FOR SELF-STUDY OR GROUP DISCUSSION

Gratitude heightens the senses as well as our awareness.

LESSON EIGHT

STEP EIGHT AND STEP NINE

Step Eight: *Made a list of all persons we had harmed, and became willing to make amends to them all.*

Step Nine: *Made direct amends to such people wherever possible, except when to do so would injure them or others.*

Up to this point we have considered and concentrated on ourselves entirely. Steps Eight and Nine take us out of our overgrown egos, and we begin to move into the wonderful world we were born into. We begin to heal and address our position with injured relationships.

First, we are asked to look back and try to discover where we may have been at fault in our dealings with others.

Second, we make vigorous attempts to repair the damage we have done.

Most of us will see a great deal of wreckage we have caused others as a result of our active addiction. We already experienced part of this when we took Step Four, but in that Step we were only concerned with ourselves. Steps Eight and Nine suggest we concentrate on others.

Most of our stories highlight a simple fact: Those we hurt the most are usually the people who love us the most.

As we look back on our behavior toward others and how it affected them, we usually see how others treated us as a result of our behavior. The focus of Step Eight is on our behavior and the responsibility that requires us to admit our wrongs.

Step Eight requires clear thinking so we can be motivated, with courage, to begin this Step.

Purposeful forgetting is a great obstacle. This is often when we are inclined to say, "I didn't hurt anyone but myself." It is important to list all infractions to anyone's integrity be it physical, emotional, or spiritual in nature. Making amends not only simply means apologies but often restitution. It is difficult to be sincere, if one is unwilling.

KEY IDEA 1

[Making amends] is a proven *way of life* by which the alcoholic corrects past mistakes and makes restitution to relatives, friends, or enemies.

HARDCOVER	PAPERBACK
PAGE 79, PARAGRAPH 2	PAGE 81, PARAGRAPH 2

SUGGESTION FOR SELF-STUDY OR GROUP DISCUSSION

It is not as important to understand how this process works at this point. We know that it works from observing the members who have taken this Step before us.

KEY IDEA 2

[Steps Eight and Nine] work in conjunction with each other.

HARDCOVER	PAPERBACK
PAGE 80, PARAGRAPH 2	PAGE 82, PARAGRAPH 3

SUGGESTION FOR SELF-STUDY OR GROUP DISCUSSION

We cannot be rid of the effects of guilt until we are aware of it, own it, and grieve it. Only then can we let it go.

STEP NINE

Made direct amends to such people wherever possible
except when to do so would injure them or others.

Qualities we need to accomplish this Step are good judgment, careful sense of timing, courage, and prudence.

There are different types of amends to be made:

1. Those to individuals who are readily available and to whom we need to make amends as soon as possible.

2. Those to whom we can only make partial restitution to, as a complete disclosure would bring harm to others or ourselves.

3. Those where action ought to be delayed at least for the time being.

4. Those we have to take a creative approach to, such as people who are unreachable or who have passed away.

5. The beginning of making amends to ourselves.

Most of us begin this Step as soon as possible after entering recovery as we demonstrate to others that we are taking action to correct negative situations caused by our behavior while under the influence. Good judgment needs to be exercised as we may rekindle arguments or try to buy peace of mind at the expense of others. We need to talk with our sponsors and fellow members about this Step.

KEY IDEA 3

Remember, in most cases you will require a lifetime to complete Step
Nine.

HARDCOVER	PAPERBACK
PAGE 81, PARAGRAPH 1	PAGE 83, PARAGRAPH 1

SUGGESTION FOR SELF-STUDY OR GROUP DISCUSSION
Another way to view procrastination is "AA begins on time and ends on
time." With our pride in balance we become more aware of the right timing in making our variety of amends.

KEY IDEA 4

Meditation and prayer are necessary to make amends.

HARDCOVER	PAPERBACK
PAGE 81, PARAGRAPH 3	PAGE 83, PARAGRAPH 3

SUGGESTION FOR SELF-STUDY OR GROUP DISCUSSION
Instead of the term *meditation*, think of "taking quiet time" for ourselves—
to reflect. In prayer, we seek courage for the confidence to take positive
action while making amends.

KEY IDEA 5

Discretion in this connection is imperative.

HARDCOVER	PAPERBACK
PAGE 81, BOTTOM	PAGE 84, TOP
PAGE 82, TOP	

SUGGESTION FOR SELF-STUDY OR GROUP DISCUSSION

The alcoholic is a self-centered individual. It is a positive learning process to be able to take other individuals' feelings into account.

Note: Read and discuss topics of these four groups: friends, families, creditors, and the deceased.

HARDCOVER	PAPERBACK
PAGES 83–88	PAGES 85–90

 **LESSON NINE**

STEP TEN

Continued to take personal inventory and when we were wrong promptly admitted it.

Step Ten tells us to put our AA way of life into everyday practice. This is a maintenance Step to ensure emotional balance. We are trying to establish the discipline of regular, daily soul-searching. We are never at a standstill. We are either moving toward a slip or away from one. This Step helps us monitor which way we are going.

Once we get a handle on the physical aspects of the disease, the danger to slack off arises. Attention must be paid to the mental and emotional aspects of the disease. Negative emotional or mental bingeing can push us toward a drink faster than a physical craving. Now that we have begun to be settled with the past, this Step anchors us in the present.

All inventories are alike in principle, but the time factor distinguishes one from another.

1. *Spot-check inventory.* This is taken at any time during the day when we feel we are getting all tangled up mentally.

2. *End of day inventory.* Here we try to balance the activities of the day—the positive and negative.

3. *Periodic inventory.* This is the updating that takes place during our frequent talks with our sponsor, spiritual advisor, or fellow members.

4. *Annual or semiannual inventory.* This is a general housecleaning, an updating of Step Four.

This practice is a valuable tool to maintain a happy and balanced recovery. Discipline is required to establish the habit of inventory taking, but once established it becomes easier and automatic.

There is a spiritual axiom that says, *Whenever I am disturbed, no matter what the cause, there is something "off the beam" with me also.* The alcoholic cannot afford the luxury of more emotionally balanced people who may live with justifiable anger and resentments. No matter how justified we may feel in indulging in these feelings, we are only victimizing ourselves and walking the dangerous road toward a relapse.

We are seeking progress not perfection. A change in our lives will gradually come, even though we may not perceive it easily.

Learning daily to be aware of, to admit, and to correct our negative qualities is the very essence of character building and contented living. An honest regret for harms done, a genuine gratitude for blessings received, and a willingness to try for better things tomorrow will yield the permanent assets we seek.

STEP TEN

DAILY INVENTORY LOG*

Use the following ratings to record your level of function each day. Ask yourself, "How am I doing (excellent, good, average, fair, poor) as I deal with _____?"

4 = Excellent   3 = Good   2 = Average   1 = Fair   0 = Poor

WEEK OF _____ _____ THROUGH _____ _____ _____
        MONTH   DAY   MONTH   DAY   YEAR

CHARACTERISTIC (LIMITATION)	MON.	TUES.	WED.	THUR.	FRI.	SAT.	SUN.
Anger/resentment							
Approval seeking							
Caretaking							
Control							
Denial							
Depression/self-pity							
Dishonesty							
Frozen feelings							
Isolation							
Jealousy							
Perfectionism							
Procrastination							
Worry (past or future)							

(continued on next page)

*More Daily Inventory Log sheets (eleven total) are located in Appendix 2 (beginning on page 93). You therefore have a log for a period of about three months.

The Little Red Book Study Guide. ©1998 by Hazelden Foundation. All rights reserved. Reproduction for personal use is permissible.

DAILY INVENTORY LOG (CONTINUED)

Ask yourself, "How am I doing (excellent, good, average, fair, poor) as I deal with _____?"

4 = Excellent   3 = Good   2 = Average   1 = Fair   0 = Poor

CHARACTERISTIC (STRENGTH)	MON.	TUES.	WED.	THUR.	FRI.	SAT.	SUN.
Forgiveness							
Generosity							
Honesty							
Humility							
Patience							
Risk-taking							
Self-nurturing							
Tolerance							
Trust							

My Notes:

_____

_____

_____

_____

_____

_____

_____

The Little Red Book Study Guide. ©1998 by Hazelden Foundation. All rights reserved. Reproduction for personal use is permissible.

My Daily Inventory*

MONTH _____ YEAR _____

INSTRUCTIONS: At the end of each day, rate areas that you need to **beware of** with an **X**, and put a ✔ next to areas in which you **made progress.**

		1	2	3	4	5	6	7	8	9	10	11	12	13	14	15	16	17	18	19	20	21	22	23	24	25	26	27	28	29	30	31
LIABILITY	SELF-PITY																															
ASSET	SELF-FORGETFULNESS																															
LIABILITY	SELF-JUSTIFICATION																															
ASSET	HUMILITY																															
LIABILITY	SELF-IMPORTANCE																															
ASSET	MODESTY																															
LIABILITY	SELF-CONDEMNATION																															
ASSET	SELF-VALUATION																															
LIABILITY	DISHONESTY																															
ASSET	HONESTY																															
LIABILITY	IMPATIENCE																															
ASSET	PATIENCE																															
LIABILITY	HATE																															
ASSET	LOVE																															
LIABILITY	RESENTMENT																															
ASSET	FORGIVENESS																															
LIABILITY	FALSE PRIDE																															
ASSET	SIMPLICITY																															
LIABILITY	JEALOUSY																															
ASSET	TRUST																															
LIABILITY	ENVY																															
ASSET	GENEROSITY																															
LIABILITY	LAZINESS																															
ASSET	ACTIVITY																															
LIABILITY	PROCRASTINATION																															
ASSET	PROMPTNESS																															
LIABILITY	INSINCERITY																															
ASSET	STRAIGHTFORWARDNESS																															
LIABILITY	NEGATIVE THINKING																															
ASSET	POSITIVE THINKING																															
LIABILITY	VULGAR, IMMORAL, TRASHY THINKING																															
ASSET	HIGH-MINDED, SPIRITUAL, CLEAN THINKING																															
LIABILITY	CRITICIZING																															
ASSET	LOOK FOR THE GOOD																															

*At the end of each month, review your chart and write a brief analysis using the worksheet on the following page. Eleven additional Daily Inventory charts and Daily Inventory Review sheets appear in appendix 3 (beginning on page 119). You therefore have a chart for every month of the year to complete.

The Little Red Book Study Guide. ©1998 by Hazelden Foundation. All rights reserved. Reproduction for personal use is permissible.

MY DAILY INVENTORY REVIEW*

MONTH _____ YEAR _____

INSTRUCTIONS: At the end of each month, review your chart and write a brief analysis below.

1. Areas in which I improved:

2. Areas in need of improvement:

3. Other goals for next month:

The Little Red Book Study Guide. ©1998 by Hazelden Foundation. All rights reserved. Reproduction for personal use is permissible.

KEY IDEA 1

AA suggests a daily inventory to disclose our harmful thoughts and actions.

HARDCOVER	PAPERBACK
PAGE 93, PARAGRAPH 1	PAGE 95, PARAGRAPH 1

SUGGESTION FOR SELF-STUDY OR GROUP DISCUSSION

Different ways of doing an inventory exist: nightly assessment or morning assessment or spot-check during the day. How to do it is not as important as doing it. We learn to grow in understanding and effectiveness.

KEY IDEA 2

"It is in man's nature that he does not stay put."

HARDCOVER	PAPERBACK
PAGE 93, PARAGRAPH 2	PAGE 95, PARAGRAPH 2

SUGGESTION FOR SELF-STUDY OR GROUP DISCUSSION

The times when we seem to be standing still are the times when we are filtering and assessing the ideas and values we pick up in AA.

KEY IDEA 3

We need daily mental checkups to announce the advent of old habits and act as sentries to detect new defects.

HARDCOVER	PAPERBACK
PAGE 95, PARAGRAPH 4	PAGE 97, BOTTOM
	PAGE 98, TOP

SUGGESTION FOR SELF-STUDY OR GROUP DISCUSSION

Acquiring positive, healing, and nurturing behavior is a discipline. If we shrink from self-examination, fear creeps back into our lives. Fear pushes out faith. Without faith we lose our recovery.

KEY IDEA 4

Our serious problem is self-centeredness.

HARDCOVER	PAPERBACK
PAGE 97, PARAGRAPH 1	PAGE 99, PARAGRAPH 2

SUGGESTION FOR SELF-STUDY OR GROUP DISCUSSION

We like to delude ourselves in thinking we are in control. Our ego fits itself to our heart and soul. If our heart and soul are in line with our Higher Power, our ego is in line.

KEY IDEA 5

The antidote is a quick review of our alcoholism.

HARDCOVER	PAPERBACK
PAGE 97, PARAGRAPH 2	PAGE 100, PARAGRAPH 1

SUGGESTION FOR SELF-STUDY OR GROUP DISCUSSION

We receive benefits when we share our stories of "what it was like, what happened, and what it's like now." When our addiction talks to us about the good times, we need to remember "the rest of the story."

KEY IDEA 6

The requirement of our program is to make amends if the wrong has harmed anyone.

HARDCOVER	PAPERBACK
PAGE 97, PARAGRAPH 2	PAGE 100, PARAGRAPH 1

SUGGESTION FOR SELF-STUDY OR GROUP DISCUSSION

There is a difference between amends and apology. We realize our character can be a force that respects truth, develops will and spirit, accents positive action, and makes all of these assets evident to other people.

Key Idea 7

It is not in the nature of the alcoholic to stay put.

Hardcover	Paperback
Page 98, Paragraph 5	Page 101, Paragraph 2

Suggestion for self-study or group discussion

There is no treading water. I am either making positive progress or moving backward. Success is simply using the abilities we have. We must treat them as practical tools, not "magical gifts." Nobody travels our road for us.

Key Idea 8

Our new personality is not compatible with moral defects or concealed errors.

Hardcover	Paperback
Page 99, Top	Page 101, Paragraph 3

Suggestion for self-study or group discussion

"We are as sick as our secrets." If we tell just one person (sponsor, doctor, and so on), it is no longer a secret. We don't want to be "sick" anymore. There can be no lies or secrets in our life of recovery. We must always be willing to be entirely honest.

KEY IDEA 9

Nothing is more important to the recovering alcoholic than the maintenance of contented sobriety.

HARDCOVER	PAPERBACK
PAGE 99, PARAGRAPH 4	PAGE 102, PARAGRAPH 1

SUGGESTION FOR SELF-STUDY OR GROUP DISCUSSION

Serenity is maintained by the daily practice of the Steps. Will we make a commitment to "take a daily inventory"?

 **LESSON TEN**

STEP ELEVEN

Sought through prayer and meditation to improve our conscious contact with God as we understood Him, praying only for knowledge of His will for us and the power to carry that out.

Prayer and meditation are the principal means we in the program use for an improved conscious contact with our Higher Power. Many members of AA are easily distracted and lose sight of priorities. Often prayer is used only in an emergency.

Just as our bodies suffer with the deprivation of food and water, so our minds and emotions suffer with the deprivation of prayer and meditation.

Memorized prayer can be helpful, but what we are after here is personal conversation with our Higher Power.

The Big Book uses the phrase "quiet time" rather than the word *meditation*. It is beneficial to set aside time during the day, usually in the morning, when we eliminate all distractions and concentrate and enjoy the sense of well-being shared with our Higher Power.

God's will for us, at any given moment, is that we experience and enjoy our full potential every day of our lives. It is then that we are in sync with God. In brief, God wants one thing only—that we be happy.

It is said that we are never burdened beyond our strength, that God will always give us the strength to cope. This Step tells us that God wants even more for us. What appears as a burden to us is only because of our tunnel vision. What we are being offered is an opportunity to grow, to expand our capacity for happiness.

Prayer and meditation is another discipline requiring commitment and consistent practice. Once established as a habit, it reaps great reward.

KEY IDEA 1

We know this Step is needed, because of the past experiences of AA members who forgot they have not been *cured* of alcoholism.

HARDCOVER	PAPERBACK
PAGE 101, PARAGRAPH 3	PAGE 103, PARAGRAPH 3

SUGGESTION FOR SELF-STUDY OR GROUP DISCUSSION

What's the difference between *recovered* and *cured*?

KEY IDEA 2

Complacency obscures the knowledge that our recovery from alcoholism was granted by a *Power greater than ourselves*.

HARDCOVER	PAPERBACK
PAGE 102, PARAGRAPH 3	PAGE 104, BOTTOM
	PAGE 105, TOP

SUGGESTION FOR SELF-STUDY OR GROUP DISCUSSION

Alcoholism is a progressive disease in all aspects—physical, mental, emotional, and spiritual.

KEY IDEA 3

In reality we are on a "daily reprieve," and our reprieves are "contingent on the maintenance of our spiritual condition."

HARDCOVER	PAPERBACK
PAGE 103, PARAGRAPH 2	PAGE 105, PARAGRAPH 3

SUGGESTION FOR SELF-STUDY OR GROUP DISCUSSION

What are the consequences of returning to a life lived on self-will?

KEY IDEA 4

A sure way of increasing this help and improving our contact with God is through simple prayers of sincere gratitude.

HARDCOVER	PAPERBACK
PAGE 103, PARAGRAPH 5	PAGE 106, TOP

SUGGESTION FOR SELF-STUDY OR GROUP DISCUSSION

Consider prayer in the context of conversation with our Higher Power.

Prayer is the means of thinking things through with your Higher Power.

KEY IDEA 5

Relaxation of mind and body and surrender of our will to God are necessary before prayer and meditation are truly satisfying.

HARDCOVER	PAPERBACK
PAGE 105, PARAGRAPH 3	PAGE 107, PARAGRAPH 3

SUGGESTION FOR SELF-STUDY OR GROUP DISCUSSION

It is important to remember the slogan: HALT—hungry, angry, lonely, tired.

KEY IDEA 6

It is simple. Try it.

HARDCOVER	PAPERBACK
PAGE 107, TOP	PAGE 109, PARAGRAPH 3

SUGGESTION FOR SELF-STUDY OR GROUP DISCUSSION

Talk the group through a meditation. What are some of the ways to relax and meditate?

KEY IDEA 7

What is God's will? How am I to know it from my own will?

HARDCOVER	PAPERBACK
PAGE 107, PARAGRAPH 3	PAGE 109, PARAGRAPH 6

SUGGESTION FOR SELF-STUDY OR GROUP DISCUSSION

If we can stay in the moment we will intuitively know what the very next thing to do is and that is all that is important. Listening for God's will for us is an ongoing practice throughout our recovery.

KEY IDEA 8

Therefore, we deduce that our understanding of God's will *starts with surrender of our wills to Him and with charitable, loving acts of service to others.*

HARDCOVER	PAPERBACK
PAGE 108, BOTTOM	PAGE 111, PARAGRAPH 1
PAGE 109, TOP	

SUGGESTION FOR SELF-STUDY OR GROUP DISCUSSION

In what ways does alcoholism produce negative, paranoid, and self-sabotaging thinking? Make a list of some examples.

KEY IDEA 9

Our efforts in this direction, aided by faith and prayer for guidance, will bring us near to God.

HARDCOVER	PAPERBACK
PAGE 109, PARAGRAPH 1	PAGE 111, BOTTOM
	PAGE 112, TOP

SUGGESTION FOR SELF-STUDY OR GROUP DISCUSSION

Just as the disease is progressive, so recovery is progressive. We also remember to take time and examine the progress we have made. Often we don't give ourselves the credit we deserve.

KEY IDEA 10

We are, to the best of our ability, gaining a knowledge of God's will by the practice of faith, honesty, and unselfish service.

HARDCOVER	PAPERBACK
PAGE 109, PARAGRAPH 2	PAGE 112, PARAGRAPH 1

SUGGESTION FOR SELF-STUDY OR GROUP DISCUSSION

Having a spiritual advisor—an objective individual who can guide us on a spiritual path—is all important.

KEY IDEA 11

They cannot be earned by merely asking. They must be earned by honest endeavor.

HARDCOVER	PAPERBACK
PAGE 110, PARAGRAPH 3	PAGE 113, PARAGRAPH 1

SUGGESTION FOR SELF-STUDY OR GROUP DISCUSSION

Easy does it—but do it.

KEY IDEA 12

It is not wise to pray for power selfishly or with resentment, envy, or self-pity in our hearts.

HARDCOVER	PAPERBACK
PAGE 111, PARAGRAPH 1	PAGE 113, PARAGRAPH 4

SUGGESTION FOR SELF-STUDY OR GROUP DISCUSSION

Our Higher Power will help us do it, but our Higher Power will not do it for us without some work on our part.

KEY IDEA 13

God releases power to those whose lives are channels for His will.

HARDCOVER	PAPERBACK
PAGE 112, PARAGRAPH 1	PAGE 114, PARAGRAPH 3

SUGGESTION FOR SELF-STUDY OR GROUP DISCUSSION

We forget about ourselves in our attempts to be of service and help others.

KEY IDEA 14

The *power to carry out God's will must come from the inspiration and energy that are found in the emotion, love—love that embraces God and humankind.*

HARDCOVER	PAPERBACK
PAGE 113, BOTTOM	PAGE 116, PARAGRAPH 4
PAGE 114, TOP	

SUGGESTION FOR SELF-STUDY OR GROUP DISCUSSION

Even though we may not "feel" love or gratitude at every given moment, that does not necessarily mean that it is not there.

 **LESSON ELEVEN**

STEP TWELVE

Having had a spiritual awakening as the result of these steps, we tried to carry this message to alcoholics, and to practice these principles in all our affairs.

It is important to remember that our program is one of attraction. We are not called upon to go out to our local saloon and recruit members. The best Twelfth Step work we can do is by example. Using the tools of the program we are called upon to go "out there" and participate in a full, rich, and creative life.

There is a danger of "hiding in the Fellowship." It is a safe and protective haven, but it is not recovery. Once we are well anchored in the program, once we have a secure foothold in reality, it is time to take risks. Often it is a trial-and-error process. Slowly we establish a new value system. We find our true identities and live them to the fullest, receiving strength and courage from our fellow members, sponsor, and Higher Power.

When going on a Twelfth Step call it is important that we not go alone. Also, it is often a waste of time to talk to someone while they are drunk. The best time is the morning after, when they are hungover and most contrite. Remember: "We carry the message—not the drunk."

Whether on a Twelfth Step call or at a meeting, always speak in the *I* forum and never in the *you*. We are to share our own strength, hope, and experience. We are not there to teach, threaten, exhort, warn, or advise. That is the area of a sponsor, therapist, counselor, or doctor. We tell our story and trust that their Higher Power will guide them to identify with us.

We did not make the person drink, nor can we make that person sober. Recovery is in the hands of that person's Higher Power. All we are called upon to do is in the footwork, and we trust the outcome to the Higher Power.

It is important to recognize and accept our own limitations. Not all are gifted in speaking to a potential new member. There are many ways to do Twelfth Step work—from setting up a hall to holding an office, or writing for the *Grapevine*; from being a sponsor to sharing at a meeting, or giving a ride to someone who needs one; from being a GSR (General Service Representative) for a group to attending AA social events, or by simply going for coffee with members after a meeting.

KEY IDEA 1

A spiritual awakening is an essential part of our recovery.

HARDCOVER	PAPERBACK
PAGE 115, PARAGRAPH 4	PAGE 119, BOTTOM
	PAGE 120, TOP

SUGGESTION FOR SELF-STUDY OR GROUP DISCUSSION

A breakthrough in denial constitutes a "spiritual awakening."

KEY IDEA 2

There would be a group of disgruntled alcoholics, temporarily on the wagon, living in a perpetual state of mental drunkenness.

HARDCOVER	PAPERBACK
PAGE 116, PARAGRAPH 1	PAGE 120, PARAGRAPH 2

SUGGESTION FOR SELF-STUDY OR GROUP DISCUSSION

How does alcoholic thinking reflect our buried feelings?

KEY IDEA 3

They had undergone a profound personality change for the better.

HARDCOVER	PAPERBACK
PAGE 117, PARAGRAPH 5	PAGE 122, PARAGRAPH 1

SUGGESTION FOR SELF-STUDY OR GROUP DISCUSSION

A change of attitude produces a personality change.

KEY IDEA 4

The quality of their sobriety does not seem important in the beginning.

HARDCOVER	PAPERBACK
PAGE 116, PARAGRAPH 1	PAGE 120, PARAGRAPH 2

SUGGESTION FOR SELF-STUDY OR GROUP DISCUSSION

People experience the "pink cloud"—the exhilaration of being physically alcohol-free.

KEY IDEA 5

They told us personalities were not changed overnight and we should be more open-minded and patient in working out the many details of our recovery.

HARDCOVER	PAPERBACK
PAGE 122, PARAGRAPH 3	PAGE 127, PARAGRAPH 2

SUGGESTION FOR SELF-STUDY OR GROUP DISCUSSION

A new value system takes time to construct. New ideas have to be weighed and measured.

KEY IDEA 6

It looks like the real thing but fails to stand up against adversity, resentment, or the physical craving for alcohol.

HARDCOVER	PAPERBACK
PAGE 123, PARAGRAPH 3	PAGE 128, PARAGRAPH 1

SUGGESTION FOR SELF-STUDY OR GROUP DISCUSSION

It is possible to "play act" recovery. We recite all the slogans and say all the things we are "supposed" to say.

KEY IDEA 7

The principle of working with others is sound, as it is founded upon the ageless axiom, "Give and you shall receive."

HARDCOVER	PAPERBACK
PAGE 129, PARAGRAPH 2	PAGE 134, PARAGRAPH 2

SUGGESTION FOR SELF-STUDY OR GROUP DISCUSSION

The more we give love, the greater our capacity to receive love increases.

KEY IDEA 8

First, they look to us for counsel to help them overcome their drinking problems; they then look to the AA program for rehabilitation of their lives.

HARDCOVER	PAPERBACK
PAGE 132, PARAGRAPH 2	PAGE 137, PARAGRAPH 2

SUGGESTION FOR SELF-STUDY OR GROUP DISCUSSION

We may feel fearful of becoming a sponsor. All that is needed is trust in one's Higher Power, knowing that the sponsee also has a Higher Power looking after him or her.

KEY IDEA 9

It is the momentary loss of self-centeredness.

HARDCOVER	PAPERBACK
PAGE 135, PARAGRAPH 2	PAGE 140, PARAGRAPH 2

SUGGESTION FOR SELF-STUDY OR GROUP DISCUSSION

We cannot feel another person's feelings. The basis of empathy is recalling similar feelings we have experienced, then understanding what the other person is going through.

KEY IDEA 10

We will avoid flooding our ranks with an unwieldy preponderance of nonalcoholics.

HARDCOVER	PAPERBACK
PAGE 137, PARAGRAPH 1	PAGE 142, PARAGRAPH 1

SUGGESTION FOR SELF-STUDY OR GROUP DISCUSSION

No one enters AA because they are healthy. Some are sicker than others.

KEY IDEA 11

If an alcoholic wants no part of AA, we can still carry the message to inquiring relatives.

HARDCOVER	PAPERBACK
PAGE 137, PARAGRAPH 2	PAGE 142, PARAGRAPH 2

SUGGESTION FOR SELF-STUDY OR GROUP DISCUSSION

Is this a disease or is it a moral issue? Why is it unreasonable to think a non-addict should understand our addiction?

KEY IDEA 12

We must protect our personal anonymity.

HARDCOVER	PAPERBACK
PAGE 138, PARAGRAPH 1	PAGE 143, PARAGRAPH 2

SUGGESTION FOR SELF-STUDY OR GROUP DISCUSSION

Motivation for disclosing one's alcoholism is highly questionable. What is the real reason we tell anyone?

KEY IDEA 13

If the alcoholic needs hospital care, help the person get it by making the necessary arrangements.

HARDCOVER	PAPERBACK
PAGE 138, PARAGRAPH 6	PAGE 144, PARAGRAPH 1

SUGGESTION FOR SELF-STUDY OR GROUP DISCUSSION

We must remember there is a very real possibility of death occurring during unmonitored detoxing.

KEY IDEA 14

It is foolish to assume you can recover from alcoholism without a book which contains the recovery instructions.

HARDCOVER	PAPERBACK
PAGE 141, PARAGRAPH 1	PAGE 146, PARAGRAPH 1

SUGGESTION FOR SELF-STUDY OR GROUP DISCUSSION

What is the difference between "being in the program or being around the program"? Have we read the Big Book?

KEY IDEA 15

Approach it with honesty, humility, open-mindedness, willingness, and appreciation.

HARDCOVER	PAPERBACK
PAGE 141, PARAGRAPH 3	PAGE 146, PARAGRAPH 3

SUGGESTION FOR SELF-STUDY OR GROUP DISCUSSION

Discuss the idea of romancing the disease.

KEY IDEA 16

The principles of the Twelve Steps add up to a logical and livable way of life which will restore health, happiness, and sobriety to sick hopeless alcoholics.

HARDCOVER	PAPERBACK
PAGE 141, PARAGRAPH 4	PAGE 146, PARAGRAPH 4

SUGGESTION FOR SELF-STUDY OR GROUP DISCUSSION

The perception of living grows larger, richer, and more abundant.

KEY IDEA 17

Hundreds of thousands of members who have recovered from alcoholism give living proof that the AA program works for those who apply it.

HARDCOVER	PAPERBACK
PAGE 141, PARAGRAPH 5	PAGE 146, PARAGRAPH 5

SUGGESTION FOR SELF-STUDY OR GROUP DISCUSSION

Give personal examples to show that the program works.

KEY IDEA 18

Seek help from God as we understand Him to arrest our spiritual illness.

HARDCOVER	PAPERBACK
PAGE 142, PARAGRAPH 3	PAGE 147, PARAGRAPH 3

SUGGESTION FOR SELF-STUDY OR GROUP DISCUSSION

Give graphic examples of your Higher Power working in your life.

KEY IDEA 19

Rely upon the Twelve Steps to inspire us with worthy motives.

HARDCOVER	PAPERBACK
PAGE 142, PARAGRAPH 3	PAGE 147, PARAGRAPH 3

SUGGESTION FOR SELF-STUDY OR GROUP DISCUSSION

Give examples of how the Twelve Steps move us into "A New Way of Life."

APPENDIX 1

THE TWELVE STEPS AND TWELVE TRADITIONS OF ALCOHOLICS ANONYMOUS

TWELVE STEPS OF ALCOHOLICS ANONYMOUS*

1. We admitted we were powerless over alcohol—that our lives had become unmanageable.

2. Came to believe that a Power greater than ourselves could restore us to sanity.

3. Made a decision to turn our will and our lives over to the care of God *as we understood Him*.

4. Made a searching and fearless moral inventory of ourselves.

5. Admitted to God, to ourselves, and to another human being the exact nature of our wrongs.

6. Were entirely ready to have God remove all these defects of character.

7. Humbly asked Him to remove our shortcomings.

8. Made a list of all persons we had harmed, and became willing to make amends to them all.

9. Made direct amends to such people wherever possible, except when to do so would injure them or others.

10. Continued to take personal inventory and when we were wrong promptly admitted it.

11. Sought through prayer and meditation to improve our conscious contact with God *as we understood Him,* praying only for knowledge of His will for us and the power to carry that out.

12. Having had a spiritual awakening as the result of these steps, we tried to carry this message to alcoholics, and to practice these principles in all our affairs.

---

*The Twelve Steps of AA are taken from *Alcoholics Anonymous*, 3d. ed., published by AA World Services, Inc., New York, N.Y., 59–60. Reprinted with permission of AA World Services, Inc. See editor's note on copyright page.

TWELVE TRADITIONS OF ALCOHOLICS ANONYMOUS*

1. Our common welfare should come first; personal recovery depends upon A.A. unity.

2. For our group purpose there is but one ultimate authority—a loving God as He may express Himself in our group conscience. Our leaders are but trusted servants; they do not govern.

3. The only requirement for A.A. membership is a desire to stop drinking.

4. Each group should be autonomous except in matters affecting other groups or A.A. as a whole.

5. Each group has but one primary purpose—to carry its message to the alcoholic who still suffers.

6. An A.A. group ought never endorse, finance, or lend the AA name to any related facility or outside enterprise, lest problems of money, property, and prestige divert us from our primary purpose.

7. Every A.A. group ought to be fully self-supporting, declining outside contributions.

8. Alcoholics Anonymous should remain forever nonprofessional, but our service centers may employ special workers.

9. A.A., as such, ought never be organized; but we may create service boards or committees directly responsible to those they serve.

10. Alcoholics Anonymous has no opinion on outside issues; hence the A.A. name ought never be drawn into public controversy.

11. Our public relations policy is based on attraction rather than promotion; we need always maintain personal anonymity at the level of press, radio, and films.

12. Anonymity is the spiritual foundation of all our traditions, ever reminding us to place principles before personalities.

*The Twelve Traditions of AA are taken from *Twelve Steps and Twelve Traditions,* published by AA World Services, Inc., New York, N.Y. Reprinted with permission of AA World Services, Inc. See editor's note on copyright page.

APPENDIX 2

DAILY INVENTORY LOGS

Step Ten

Daily Inventory Log*

Use the following ratings to record your level of function each day. Ask yourself, "How am I doing (excellent, good, average, fair, poor) as I deal with _____?"

4 = Excellent   3 = Good   2 = Average   1 = Fair   0 = Poor

Week of _____ _____ Through _____ _____ _____
              Month   Day   Month   Day   Year

Characteristic (limitation)	Mon.	Tues.	Wed.	Thur.	Fri.	Sat.	Sun.
Anger/resentment							
Approval seeking							
Caretaking							
Control							
Denial							
Depression/self-pity							
Dishonesty							
Frozen feelings							
Isolation							
Jealousy							
Perfectionism							
Procrastination							
Worry (past or future)							

(continued on next page)

The Little Red Book Study Guide. ©1998 by Hazelden Foundation. All rights reserved. Reproduction for personal use is permissible.

Daily Inventory Log (continued)

Ask yourself, "How am I doing (excellent, good, average, fair, poor) as I deal with _____?"

4 = Excellent 3 = Good 2 = Average 1 = Fair 0 = Poor

Characteristic (Strength)	Mon.	Tues.	Wed.	Thur.	Fri.	Sat.	Sun.
Forgiveness							
Generosity							
Honesty							
Humility							
Patience							
Risk-taking							
Self-nurturing							
Tolerance							
Trust							

My Notes:

_____

_____

_____

_____

_____

_____

_____

The Little Red Book Study Guide. ©1998 by Hazelden Foundation. All rights reserved. Reproduction for personal use is permissible.

STEP TEN

DAILY INVENTORY LOG*

Use the following ratings to record your level of function each day. Ask yourself, "How am I doing (excellent, good, average, fair, poor) as I deal with _____?"

4 = Excellent   3 = Good   2 = Average   1 = Fair   0 = Poor

WEEK OF _____ ____ THROUGH _____ ____ _____
         MONTH   DAY   MONTH   DAY   YEAR

CHARACTERISTIC (LIMITATION)	MON.	TUES.	WED.	THUR.	FRI.	SAT.	SUN.
Anger/resentment							
Approval seeking							
Caretaking							
Control							
Denial							
Depression/self-pity							
Dishonesty							
Frozen feelings							
Isolation							
Jealousy							
Perfectionism							
Procrastination							
Worry (past or future)							

(continued on next page)

The Little Red Book Study Guide. ©1998 by Hazelden Foundation. All rights reserved. Reproduction for personal use is permissible.

Daily Inventory Log (continued)

Ask yourself, "How am I doing (excellent, good, average, fair, poor) as I deal with _____?"

4 = Excellent   3 = Good   2 = Average   1 = Fair   0 = Poor

Characteristic (Strength)	Mon.	Tues.	Wed.	Thur.	Fri.	Sat.	Sun.
Forgiveness							
Generosity							
Honesty							
Humility							
Patience							
Risk-taking							
Self-nurturing							
Tolerance							
Trust							

My Notes:

_____

_____

_____

_____

_____

_____

_____

The Little Red Book Study Guide. ©1998 by Hazelden Foundation. All rights reserved. Reproduction for personal use is permissible.

STEP TEN

DAILY INVENTORY LOG*

Use the following ratings to record your level of function each day. Ask yourself, "How am I doing (excellent, good, average, fair, poor) as I deal with _____?"

4 = Excellent   3 = Good   2 = Average   1 = Fair   0 = Poor

WEEK OF _____ ____ THROUGH _____ ____ ____
        MONTH   DAY   MONTH   DAY YEAR

CHARACTERISTIC (LIMITATION)	MON.	TUES.	WED.	THUR.	FRI.	SAT.	SUN.
Anger/resentment							
Approval seeking							
Caretaking							
Control							
Denial							
Depression/self-pity							
Dishonesty							
Frozen feelings							
Isolation							
Jealousy							
Perfectionism							
Procrastination							
Worry (past or future)							

(continued on next page)

The Little Red Book Study Guide. ©1998 by Hazelden Foundation. All rights reserved. Reproduction for personal use is permissible.

DAILY INVENTORY LOG (CONTINUED)

Ask yourself, "How am I doing (excellent, good, average, fair, poor) as I deal with _____?"

4 = Excellent   3 = Good   2 = Average   1 = Fair   0 = Poor

CHARACTERISTIC (STRENGTH)	MON.	TUES.	WED.	THUR.	FRI.	SAT.	SUN.
Forgiveness							
Generosity							
Honesty							
Humility							
Patience							
Risk-taking							
Self-nurturing							
Tolerance							
Trust							

My Notes:

_____

_____

_____

_____

_____

_____

_____

The Little Red Book Study Guide. ©1998 by Hazelden Foundation. All rights reserved. Reproduction for personal use is permissible.

STEP TEN

DAILY INVENTORY LOG*

Use the following ratings to record your level of function each day. Ask yourself, "How am I doing (excellent, good, average, fair, poor) as I deal with _____?"

4 = Excellent   3 = Good   2 = Average   1 = Fair   0 = Poor

WEEK OF _____ _____ THROUGH _____ _____ _____
        MONTH   DAY   MONTH   DAY   YEAR

CHARACTERISTIC (LIMITATION)	MON.	TUES.	WED.	THUR.	FRI.	SAT.	SUN.
Anger/resentment							
Approval seeking							
Caretaking							
Control							
Denial							
Depression/self-pity							
Dishonesty							
Frozen feelings							
Isolation							
Jealousy							
Perfectionism							
Procrastination							
Worry (past or future)							

(continued on next page)

The Little Red Book Study Guide. ©1998 by Hazelden Foundation. All rights reserved. Reproduction for personal use is permissible.

DAILY INVENTORY LOG (CONTINUED)

Ask yourself, "How am I doing (excellent, good, average, fair, poor) as I deal with _____?"

4 = Excellent   3 = Good   2 = Average   1 = Fair   0 = Poor

CHARACTERISTIC (STRENGTH)	MON.	TUES.	WED.	THUR.	FRI.	SAT.	SUN.
Forgiveness							
Generosity							
Honesty							
Humility							
Patience							
Risk-taking							
Self-nurturing							
Tolerance							
Trust							

My Notes:

_____

_____

_____

_____

_____

_____

_____

The Little Red Book Study Guide. ©1998 by Hazelden Foundation. All rights reserved. Reproduction for personal use is permissible.

Step Ten

Daily Inventory Log*

Use the following ratings to record your level of function each day. Ask yourself, "How am I doing (excellent, good, average, fair, poor) as I deal with _____?"

4 = Excellent   3 = Good   2 = Average   1 = Fair   0 = Poor

Week of _____ _____ Through _____ _____ _____
            Month   Day   Month   Day   Year

Characteristic (limitation)	Mon.	Tues.	Wed.	Thur.	Fri.	Sat.	Sun.
Anger/resentment							
Approval seeking							
Caretaking							
Control							
Denial							
Depression/self-pity							
Dishonesty							
Frozen feelings							
Isolation							
Jealousy							
Perfectionism							
Procrastination							
Worry (past or future)							

(continued on next page)

The Little Red Book Study Guide. ©1998 by Hazelden Foundation. All rights reserved. Reproduction for personal use is permissible.

Daily Inventory Log (continued)

Ask yourself, "How am I doing (excellent, good, average, fair, poor) as I deal with _____?"

4 = Excellent   3 = Good   2 = Average   1 = Fair   0 = Poor

Characteristic (Strength)	Mon.	Tues.	Wed.	Thur.	Fri.	Sat.	Sun.
Forgiveness							
Generosity							
Honesty							
Humility							
Patience							
Risk-taking							
Self-nurturing							
Tolerance							
Trust							

My Notes:

_____

_____

_____

_____

_____

_____

_____

The Little Red Book Study Guide. ©1998 by Hazelden Foundation. All rights reserved. Reproduction for personal use is permissible.

STEP TEN

DAILY INVENTORY LOG*

Use the following ratings to record your level of function each day. Ask yourself, "How am I doing (excellent, good, average, fair, poor) as I deal with _____?"

4 = Excellent   3 = Good   2 = Average   1 = Fair   0 = Poor

WEEK OF _____ ____ THROUGH _____ ____ ____
             MONTH   DAY   MONTH   DAY   YEAR

CHARACTERISTIC (LIMITATION)	MON.	TUES.	WED.	THUR.	FRI.	SAT.	SUN.
Anger/resentment							
Approval seeking							
Caretaking							
Control							
Denial							
Depression/self-pity							
Dishonesty							
Frozen feelings							
Isolation							
Jealousy							
Perfectionism							
Procrastination							
Worry (past or future)							

(continued on next page)

The Little Red Book Study Guide. ©1998 by Hazelden Foundation. All rights reserved. Reproduction for personal use is permissible.

DAILY INVENTORY LOG (CONTINUED)

Ask yourself, "How am I doing (excellent, good, average, fair, poor) as I deal with _____?"

4 = Excellent   3 = Good   2 = Average   1 = Fair   0 = Poor

CHARACTERISTIC (STRENGTH)	MON.	TUES.	WED.	THUR.	FRI.	SAT.	SUN.
Forgiveness							
Generosity							
Honesty							
Humility							
Patience							
Risk-taking							
Self-nurturing							
Tolerance							
Trust							

My Notes:

_____

_____

_____

_____

_____

_____

_____

The Little Red Book Study Guide. ©1998 by Hazelden Foundation. All rights reserved. Reproduction for personal use is permissible.

STEP TEN

DAILY INVENTORY LOG*

Use the following ratings to record your level of function each day. Ask yourself, "How am I doing (excellent, good, average, fair, poor) as I deal with _____?"

4 = Excellent   3 = Good   2 = Average   1 = Fair   0 = Poor

WEEK OF _____ ____ THROUGH _____ ____ ____
MONTH DAY   MONTH   DAY   YEAR

CHARACTERISTIC (LIMITATION)	MON.	TUES.	WED.	THUR.	FRI.	SAT.	SUN.
Anger/resentment							
Approval seeking							
Caretaking							
Control							
Denial							
Depression/self-pity							
Dishonesty							
Frozen feelings							
Isolation							
Jealousy							
Perfectionism							
Procrastination							
Worry (past or future)							

(continued on next page)

The Little Red Book Study Guide. ©1998 by Hazelden Foundation. All rights reserved. Reproduction for personal use is permissible.

DAILY INVENTORY LOG (CONTINUED)

Ask yourself, "How am I doing (excellent, good, average, fair, poor) as I deal with _____?"

4 = Excellent   3 = Good   2 = Average   1 = Fair   0 = Poor

CHARACTERISTIC (STRENGTH)	MON.	TUES.	WED.	THUR.	FRI.	SAT.	SUN.
Forgiveness							
Generosity							
Honesty							
Humility							
Patience							
Risk-taking							
Self-nurturing							
Tolerance							
Trust							

My Notes:

_____

_____

_____

_____

_____

_____

_____

The Little Red Book Study Guide. ©1998 by Hazelden Foundation. All rights reserved. Reproduction for personal use is permissible.

STEP TEN

DAILY INVENTORY LOG*

Use the following ratings to record your level of function each day. Ask yourself, "How am I doing (excellent, good, average, fair, poor) as I deal with _____?"

4 = Excellent   3 = Good   2 = Average   1 = Fair   0 = Poor

WEEK OF _____ _____   THROUGH _____ _____ _____
MONTH   DAY   MONTH   DAY   YEAR

CHARACTERISTIC (LIMITATION)	MON.	TUES.	WED.	THUR.	FRI.	SAT.	SUN.
Anger/resentment							
Approval seeking							
Caretaking							
Control							
Denial							
Depression/self-pity							
Dishonesty							
Frozen feelings							
Isolation							
Jealousy							
Perfectionism							
Procrastination							
Worry (past or future)							

(continued on next page)

The Little Red Book Study Guide. ©1998 by Hazelden Foundation. All rights reserved. Reproduction for personal use is permissible.

DAILY INVENTORY LOG (CONTINUED)

Ask yourself, "How am I doing (excellent, good, average, fair, poor) as I deal with _____?"

4 = Excellent   3 = Good   2 = Average   1 = Fair   0 = Poor

CHARACTERISTIC (STRENGTH)	MON.	TUES.	WED.	THUR.	FRI.	SAT.	SUN.
Forgiveness							
Generosity							
Honesty							
Humility							
Patience							
Risk-taking							
Self-nurturing							
Tolerance							
Trust							

My Notes:

_____

_____

_____

_____

_____

_____

_____

The Little Red Book Study Guide. ©1998 by Hazelden Foundation. All rights reserved. Reproduction for personal use is permissible.

STEP TEN

DAILY INVENTORY LOG*

Use the following ratings to record your level of function each day. Ask yourself, "How am I doing (excellent, good, average, fair, poor) as I deal with _____?"

4 = Excellent   3 = Good   2 = Average   1 = Fair   0 = Poor

WEEK OF _____ ____ THROUGH _____ ____ ____
          MONTH   DAY   MONTH   DAY YEAR

CHARACTERISTIC (LIMITATION)	MON.	TUES.	WED.	THUR.	FRI.	SAT.	SUN.
Anger/resentment							
Approval seeking							
Caretaking							
Control							
Denial							
Depression/self-pity							
Dishonesty							
Frozen feelings							
Isolation							
Jealousy							
Perfectionism							
Procrastination							
Worry (past or future)							

(continued on next page)

The Little Red Book Study Guide. ©1998 by Hazelden Foundation. All rights reserved. Reproduction for personal use is permissible.

Daily Inventory Log (continued)

Ask yourself, "How am I doing (excellent, good, average, fair, poor) as I deal with _____?"

4 = Excellent   3 = Good   2 = Average   1 = Fair   0 = Poor

CHARACTERISTIC (STRENGTH)	MON.	TUES.	WED.	THUR.	FRI.	SAT.	SUN.
Forgiveness							
Generosity							
Honesty							
Humility							
Patience							
Risk-taking							
Self-nurturing							
Tolerance							
Trust							

My Notes:

_____

_____

_____

_____

_____

_____

_____

The Little Red Book Study Guide. ©1998 by Hazelden Foundation. All rights reserved. Reproduction for personal use is permissible.

STEP TEN

DAILY INVENTORY LOG*

Use the following ratings to record your level of function each day. Ask yourself, "How am I doing (excellent, good, average, fair, poor) as I deal with _____?"

4 = Excellent   3 = Good   2 = Average   1 = Fair   0 = Poor

WEEK OF _____ _____ THROUGH _____ _____ _____
MONTH   DAY   MONTH   DAY   YEAR

CHARACTERISTIC (LIMITATION)	MON.	TUES.	WED.	THUR.	FRI.	SAT.	SUN.
Anger/resentment							
Approval seeking							
Caretaking							
Control							
Denial							
Depression/self-pity							
Dishonesty							
Frozen feelings							
Isolation							
Jealousy							
Perfectionism							
Procrastination							
Worry (past or future)							

(continued on next page)

The Little Red Book Study Guide. ©1998 by Hazelden Foundation. All rights reserved. Reproduction for personal use is permissible.

Daily Inventory Log (continued)

Ask yourself, "How am I doing (excellent, good, average, fair, poor) as I deal with _____?"

4 = Excellent   3 = Good   2 = Average   1 = Fair   0 = Poor

Characteristic (Strength)	Mon.	Tues.	Wed.	Thur.	Fri.	Sat.	Sun.
Forgiveness							
Generosity							
Honesty							
Humility							
Patience							
Risk-taking							
Self-nurturing							
Tolerance							
Trust							

My Notes:

_____

_____

_____

_____

_____

_____

_____

The Little Red Book Study Guide. ©1998 by Hazelden Foundation. All rights reserved. Reproduction for personal use is permissible.

STEP TEN

DAILY INVENTORY LOG*

Use the following ratings to record your level of function each day. Ask yourself, "How am I doing (excellent, good, average, fair, poor) as I deal with _____?"

4 = Excellent   3 = Good   2 = Average   1 = Fair   0 = Poor

WEEK OF _____ _____ THROUGH _____ _____ _____
          MONTH   DAY   MONTH   DAY   YEAR

CHARACTERISTIC (LIMITATION)	MON.	TUES.	WED.	THUR.	FRI.	SAT.	SUN.
Anger/resentment							
Approval seeking							
Caretaking							
Control							
Denial							
Depression/self-pity							
Dishonesty							
Frozen feelings							
Isolation							
Jealousy							
Perfectionism							
Procrastination							
Worry (past or future)							

(continued on next page)

The Little Red Book Study Guide. ©1998 by Hazelden Foundation. All rights reserved. Reproduction for personal use is permissible.

Daily Inventory Log (continued)

Ask yourself, "How am I doing (excellent, good, average, fair, poor) as I deal with _____?"

4 = Excellent 3 = Good 2 = Average 1 = Fair 0 = Poor

CHARACTERISTIC (STRENGTH)	MON.	TUES.	WED.	THUR.	FRI.	SAT.	SUN.
Forgiveness							
Generosity							
Honesty							
Humility							
Patience							
Risk-taking							
Self-nurturing							
Tolerance							
Trust							

My Notes:

_____

_____

_____

_____

_____

_____

_____

_____

The Little Red Book Study Guide. ©1998 by Hazelden Foundation. All rights reserved. Reproduction for personal use is permissible.

APPENDIX 3

MY DAILY INVENTORY

MY DAILY INVENTORY*

MONTH _____ YEAR _____

INSTRUCTIONS: At the end of each day, rate areas that you need to **beware of** with an **X**, and put a ✔ next to areas in which you **made progress**.

		1	2	3	4	5	6	7	8	9	10	11	12	13	14	15	16	17	18	19	20	21	22	23	24	25	26	27	28	29	30	31
LIABILITY	SELF-PITY																															
ASSET	SELF-FORGETFULNESS																															
LIABILITY	SELF-JUSTIFICATION																															
ASSET	HUMILITY																															
LIABILITY	SELF-IMPORTANCE																															
ASSET	MODESTY																															
LIABILITY	SELF-CONDEMNATION																															
ASSET	SELF-VALUATION																															
LIABILITY	DISHONESTY																															
ASSET	HONESTY																															
LIABILITY	IMPATIENCE																															
ASSET	PATIENCE																															
LIABILITY	HATE																															
ASSET	LOVE																															
LIABILITY	RESENTMENT																															
ASSET	FORGIVENESS																															
LIABILITY	FALSE PRIDE																															
ASSET	SIMPLICITY																															
LIABILITY	JEALOUSY																															
ASSET	TRUST																															
LIABILITY	ENVY																															
ASSET	GENEROSITY																															
LIABILITY	LAZINESS																															
ASSET	ACTIVITY																															
LIABILITY	PROCRASTINATION																															
ASSET	PROMPTNESS																															
LIABILITY	INSINCERITY																															
ASSET	STRAIGHTFORWARDNESS																															
LIABILITY	NEGATIVE THINKING																															
ASSET	POSITIVE THINKING																															
LIABILITY	VULGAR, IMMORAL, TRASHY THINKING																															
ASSET	HIGH-MINDED, SPIRITUAL, CLEAN THINKING																															
LIABILITY	CRITICIZING																															
ASSET	LOOK FOR THE GOOD																															

*At the end of each month, review your chart and write a brief analysis using the worksheet on the following page.

The Little Red Book Study Guide. ©1998 by Hazelden Foundation. All rights reserved. Reproduction for personal use is permissible.

MY DAILY INVENTORY REVIEW*

MONTH _____ YEAR _____

INSTRUCTIONS: At the end of each month, review your chart and write a brief analysis below.

1. Areas in which I improved:

_____

_____

_____

_____

_____

2. Areas in need of improvement:

_____

_____

_____

_____

_____

3. Other goals for next month:

_____

_____

_____

_____

_____

The Little Red Book Study Guide. ©1998 by Hazelden Foundation. All rights reserved. Reproduction for personal use is permissible.

MY DAILY INVENTORY*

MONTH _____ YEAR _____

INSTRUCTIONS: At the end of each day, rate areas that you need to **beware of** with an **X**, and put a ✔ next to areas in which you **made progress.**

		1	2	3	4	5	6	7	8	9	10	11	12	13	14	15	16	17	18	19	20	21	22	23	24	25	26	27	28	29	30	31
LIABILITY	SELF-PITY																															
ASSET	SELF-FORGETFULNESS																															
LIABILITY	SELF-JUSTIFICATION																															
ASSET	HUMILITY																															
LIABILITY	SELF-IMPORTANCE																															
ASSET	MODESTY																															
LIABILITY	SELF-CONDEMNATION																															
ASSET	SELF-VALUATION																															
LIABILITY	DISHONESTY																															
ASSET	HONESTY																															
LIABILITY	IMPATIENCE																															
ASSET	PATIENCE																															
LIABILITY	HATE																															
ASSET	LOVE																															
LIABILITY	RESENTMENT																															
ASSET	FORGIVENESS																															
LIABILITY	FALSE PRIDE																															
ASSET	SIMPLICITY																															
LIABILITY	JEALOUSY																															
ASSET	TRUST																															
LIABILITY	ENVY																															
ASSET	GENEROSITY																															
LIABILITY	LAZINESS																															
ASSET	ACTIVITY																															
LIABILITY	PROCRASTINATION																															
ASSET	PROMPTNESS																															
LIABILITY	INSINCERITY																															
ASSET	STRAIGHTFORWARDNESS																															
LIABILITY	NEGATIVE THINKING																															
ASSET	POSITIVE THINKING																															
LIABILITY	VULGAR, IMMORAL, TRASHY THINKING																															
ASSET	HIGH-MINDED, SPIRITUAL, CLEAN THINKING																															
LIABILITY	CRITICIZING																															
ASSET	LOOK FOR THE GOOD																															

*At the end of each month, review your chart and write a brief analysis using the worksheet on the following page.

The Little Red Book Study Guide. ©1998 by Hazelden Foundation. All rights reserved. Reproduction for personal use is permissible.

MY DAILY INVENTORY REVIEW*

MONTH _____ YEAR _____

INSTRUCTIONS: At the end of each month, review your chart and write a brief analysis below.

1. Areas in which I improved:

_____

_____

_____

_____

_____

2. Areas in need of improvement:

_____

_____

_____

_____

3. Other goals for next month:

_____

_____

_____

_____

_____

The Little Red Book Study Guide. ©1998 by Hazelden Foundation. All rights reserved. Reproduction for personal use is permissible.

MY DAILY INVENTORY*

MONTH _____ **YEAR** _____

INSTRUCTIONS: At the end of each day, rate areas that you need to **beware of** with an **X**, and put a ✔ next to areas in which you **made progress.**

		1	2	3	4	5	6	7	8	9	10	11	12	13	14	15	16	17	18	19	20	21	22	23	24	25	26	27	28	29	30	31
LIABILITY	SELF-PITY																															
ASSET	SELF-FORGETFULNESS																															
LIABILITY	SELF-JUSTIFICATION																															
ASSET	HUMILITY																															
LIABILITY	SELF-IMPORTANCE																															
ASSET	MODESTY																															
LIABILITY	SELF-CONDEMNATION																															
ASSET	SELF-VALUATION																															
LIABILITY	DISHONESTY																															
ASSET	HONESTY																															
LIABILITY	IMPATIENCE																															
ASSET	PATIENCE																															
LIABILITY	HATE																															
ASSET	LOVE																															
LIABILITY	RESENTMENT																															
ASSET	FORGIVENESS																															
LIABILITY	FALSE PRIDE																															
ASSET	SIMPLICITY																															
LIABILITY	JEALOUSY																															
ASSET	TRUST																															
LIABILITY	ENVY																															
ASSET	GENEROSITY																															
LIABILITY	LAZINESS																															
ASSET	ACTIVITY																															
LIABILITY	PROCRASTINATION																															
ASSET	PROMPTNESS																															
LIABILITY	INSINCERITY																															
ASSET	STRAIGHTFORWARDNESS																															
LIABILITY	NEGATIVE THINKING																															
ASSET	POSITIVE THINKING																															
LIABILITY	VULGAR, IMMORAL, TRASHY THINKING																															
ASSET	HIGH-MINDED, SPIRITUAL, CLEAN THINKING																															
LIABILITY	CRITICIZING																															
ASSET	LOOK FOR THE GOOD																															

*At the end of each month, review your chart and write a brief analysis using the worksheet on the following page.

The Little Red Book Study Guide. ©1998 by Hazelden Foundation. All rights reserved. Reproduction for personal use is permissible.

MY DAILY INVENTORY REVIEW*

MONTH _____ YEAR _____

INSTRUCTIONS: At the end of each month, review your chart and write a brief analysis below.

1. Areas in which I improved:

_____

_____

_____

_____

_____

2. Areas in need of improvement:

_____

_____

_____

_____

_____

3. Other goals for next month:

_____

_____

_____

_____

_____

The Little Red Book Study Guide. ©1998 by Hazelden Foundation. All rights reserved. Reproduction for personal use is permissible.

MY DAILY INVENTORY*

MONTH _____ YEAR _____

INSTRUCTIONS: At the end of each day, rate areas that you need to **beware of** with an X, and put a ✔ next to areas in which you **made progress.**

		1	2	3	4	5	6	7	8	9	10	11	12	13	14	15	16	17	18	19	20	21	22	23	24	25	26	27	28	29	30	31
LIABILITY	SELF-PITY																															
ASSET	SELF-FORGETFULNESS																															
LIABILITY	SELF-JUSTIFICATION																															
ASSET	HUMILITY																															
LIABILITY	SELF-IMPORTANCE																															
ASSET	MODESTY																															
LIABILITY	SELF-CONDEMNATION																															
ASSET	SELF-VALUATION																															
LIABILITY	DISHONESTY																															
ASSET	HONESTY																															
LIABILITY	IMPATIENCE																															
ASSET	PATIENCE																															
LIABILITY	HATE																															
ASSET	LOVE																															
LIABILITY	RESENTMENT																															
ASSET	FORGIVENESS																															
LIABILITY	FALSE PRIDE																															
ASSET	SIMPLICITY																															
LIABILITY	JEALOUSY																															
ASSET	TRUST																															
LIABILITY	ENVY																															
ASSET	GENEROSITY																															
LIABILITY	LAZINESS																															
ASSET	ACTIVITY																															
LIABILITY	PROCRASTINATION																															
ASSET	PROMPTNESS																															
LIABILITY	INSINCERITY																															
ASSET	STRAIGHTFORWARDNESS																															
LIABILITY	NEGATIVE THINKING																															
ASSET	POSITIVE THINKING																															
LIABILITY	VULGAR, IMMORAL, TRASHY THINKING																															
ASSET	HIGH-MINDED, SPIRITUAL, CLEAN THINKING																															
LIABILITY	CRITICIZING																															
ASSET	LOOK FOR THE GOOD																															

*At the end of each month, review your chart and write a brief analysis using the worksheet on the following page.

The Little Red Book Study Guide. ©1998 by Hazelden Foundation. All rights reserved. Reproduction for personal use is permissible.

MY DAILY INVENTORY REVIEW*

MONTH _____ YEAR _____

INSTRUCTIONS: At the end of each month, review your chart and write a brief analysis below.

1. Areas in which I improved:

_____

_____

_____

_____

2. Areas in need of improvement:

_____

_____

_____

_____

3. Other goals for next month:

_____

_____

_____

_____

The Little Red Book Study Guide. ©1998 by Hazelden Foundation. All rights reserved. Reproduction for personal use is permissible.

MY DAILY INVENTORY*

MONTH _____   YEAR _____

INSTRUCTIONS: At the end of each day, rate areas that you need to **beware of** with an **X**, and put a ✔ next to areas in which you **made progress.**

		1	2	3	4	5	6	7	8	9	10	11	12	13	14	15	16	17	18	19	20	21	22	23	24	25	26	27	28	29	30	31
LIABILITY	SELF-PITY																															
ASSET	SELF-FORGETFULNESS																															
LIABILITY	SELF-JUSTIFICATION																															
ASSET	HUMILITY																															
LIABILITY	SELF-IMPORTANCE																															
ASSET	MODESTY																															
LIABILITY	SELF-CONDEMNATION																															
ASSET	SELF-VALUATION																															
LIABILITY	DISHONESTY																															
ASSET	HONESTY																															
LIABILITY	IMPATIENCE																															
ASSET	PATIENCE																															
LIABILITY	HATE																															
ASSET	LOVE																															
LIABILITY	RESENTMENT																															
ASSET	FORGIVENESS																															
LIABILITY	FALSE PRIDE																															
ASSET	SIMPLICITY																															
LIABILITY	JEALOUSY																															
ASSET	TRUST																															
LIABILITY	ENVY																															
ASSET	GENEROSITY																															
LIABILITY	LAZINESS																															
ASSET	ACTIVITY																															
LIABILITY	PROCRASTINATION																															
ASSET	PROMPTNESS																															
LIABILITY	INSINCERITY																															
ASSET	STRAIGHTFORWARDNESS																															
LIABILITY	NEGATIVE THINKING																															
ASSET	POSITIVE THINKING																															
LIABILITY	VULGAR, IMMORAL, TRASHY THINKING																															
ASSET	HIGH-MINDED, SPIRITUAL, CLEAN THINKING																															
LIABILITY	CRITICIZING																															
ASSET	LOOK FOR THE GOOD																															

*At the end of each month, review your chart and write a brief analysis using the worksheet on the following page.

The Little Red Book Study Guide. ©1998 by Hazelden Foundation. All rights reserved. Reproduction for personal use is permissible.

MY DAILY INVENTORY REVIEW*

MONTH _____ YEAR _____

INSTRUCTIONS: At the end of each month, review your chart and write a brief analysis below.

1. Areas in which I improved:

_____

_____

_____

_____

_____

2. Areas in need of improvement:

_____

_____

_____

_____

_____

3. Other goals for next month:

_____

_____

_____

_____

_____

The Little Red Book Study Guide. ©1998 by Hazelden Foundation. All rights reserved. Reproduction for personal use is permissible.

MY DAILY INVENTORY*

MONTH _____ YEAR _____

INSTRUCTIONS: At the end of each day, rate areas that you need to beware of with an **X**, and put a ✔ next to areas in which you **made progress**.

		1	2	3	4	5	6	7	8	9	10	11	12	13	14	15	16	17	18	19	20	21	22	23	24	25	26	27	28	29	30	31
LIABILITY	SELF-PITY																															
ASSET	SELF-FORGETFULNESS																															
LIABILITY	SELF-JUSTIFICATION																															
ASSET	HUMILITY																															
LIABILITY	SELF-IMPORTANCE																															
ASSET	MODESTY																															
LIABILITY	SELF-CONDEMNATION																															
ASSET	SELF-VALUATION																															
LIABILITY	DISHONESTY																															
ASSET	HONESTY																															
LIABILITY	IMPATIENCE																															
ASSET	PATIENCE																															
LIABILITY	HATE																															
ASSET	LOVE																															
LIABILITY	RESENTMENT																															
ASSET	FORGIVENESS																															
LIABILITY	FALSE PRIDE																															
ASSET	SIMPLICITY																															
LIABILITY	JEALOUSY																															
ASSET	TRUST																															
LIABILITY	ENVY																															
ASSET	GENEROSITY																															
LIABILITY	LAZINESS																															
ASSET	ACTIVITY																															
LIABILITY	PROCRASTINATION																															
ASSET	PROMPTNESS																															
LIABILITY	INSINCERITY																															
ASSET	STRAIGHTFORWARDNESS																															
LIABILITY	NEGATIVE THINKING																															
ASSET	POSITIVE THINKING																															
LIABILITY	VULGAR, IMMORAL, TRASHY THINKING																															
ASSET	HIGH-MINDED, SPIRITUAL, CLEAN THINKING																															
LIABILITY	CRITICIZING																															
ASSET	LOOK FOR THE GOOD																															

*At the end of each month, review your chart and write a brief analysis using the worksheet on the following page.

The Little Red Book Study Guide. ©1998 by Hazelden Foundation. All rights reserved. Reproduction for personal use is permissible.

MY DAILY INVENTORY REVIEW*

MONTH _____ YEAR _____

INSTRUCTIONS: At the end of each month, review your chart and write a brief analysis below.

1. Areas in which I improved:

_____

_____

_____

_____

_____

_____

2. Areas in need of improvement:

_____

_____

_____

_____

_____

3. Other goals for next month:

_____

_____

_____

_____

_____

The Little Red Book Study Guide. ©1998 by Hazelden Foundation. All rights reserved. Reproduction for personal use is permissible.

MY DAILY INVENTORY*

MONTH _____ YEAR _____

INSTRUCTIONS: At the end of each day, rate areas that you need to **beware of** with an **X**, and put a ✔ next to areas in which you **made progress.**

		1	2	3	4	5	6	7	8	9	10	11	12	13	14	15	16	17	18	19	20	21	22	23	24	25	26	27	28	29	30	31
LIABILITY	SELF-PITY																															
ASSET	SELF-FORGETFULNESS																															
LIABILITY	SELF-JUSTIFICATION																															
ASSET	HUMILITY																															
LIABILITY	SELF-IMPORTANCE																															
ASSET	MODESTY																															
LIABILITY	SELF-CONDEMNATION																															
ASSET	SELF-VALUATION																															
LIABILITY	DISHONESTY																															
ASSET	HONESTY																															
LIABILITY	IMPATIENCE																															
ASSET	PATIENCE																															
LIABILITY	HATE																															
ASSET	LOVE																															
LIABILITY	RESENTMENT																															
ASSET	FORGIVENESS																															
LIABILITY	FALSE PRIDE																															
ASSET	SIMPLICITY																															
LIABILITY	JEALOUSY																															
ASSET	TRUST																															
LIABILITY	ENVY																															
ASSET	GENEROSITY																															
LIABILITY	LAZINESS																															
ASSET	ACTIVITY																															
LIABILITY	PROCRASTINATION																															
ASSET	PROMPTNESS																															
LIABILITY	INSINCERITY																															
ASSET	STRAIGHTFORWARDNESS																															
LIABILITY	NEGATIVE THINKING																															
ASSET	POSITIVE THINKING																															
LIABILITY	VULGAR, IMMORAL, TRASHY THINKING																															
ASSET	HIGH-MINDED, SPIRITUAL, CLEAN THINKING																															
LIABILITY	CRITICIZING																															
ASSET	LOOK FOR THE GOOD																															

*At the end of each month, review your chart and write a brief analysis using the worksheet on the following page.

The Little Red Book Study Guide. ©1998 by Hazelden Foundation. All rights reserved. Reproduction for personal use is permissible.

MY DAILY INVENTORY REVIEW*

MONTH _____ YEAR _____

INSTRUCTIONS: At the end of each month, review your chart and write a brief analysis below.

1. Areas in which I improved:

_____
_____
_____
_____

2. Areas in need of improvement:

_____
_____
_____
_____

3. Other goals for next month:

_____
_____
_____
_____

*The Little Red Book Study Guide. ©1998 by Hazelden Foundation. All rights reserved. Reproduction for personal use is permissible.

MY DAILY INVENTORY* MONTH _____ YEAR _____

INSTRUCTIONS: At the end of each day, rate areas that you need to **beware of** with an **X**, and put a ✔ next to areas in which you **made progress.**

		1	2	3	4	5	6	7	8	9	10	11	12	13	14	15	16	17	18	19	20	21	22	23	24	25	26	27	28	29	30	31
LIABILITY	SELF-PITY																															
ASSET	SELF-FORGETFULNESS																															
LIABILITY	SELF-JUSTIFICATION																															
ASSET	HUMILITY																															
LIABILITY	SELF-IMPORTANCE																															
ASSET	MODESTY																															
LIABILITY	SELF-CONDEMNATION																															
ASSET	SELF-VALUATION																															
LIABILITY	DISHONESTY																															
ASSET	HONESTY																															
LIABILITY	IMPATIENCE																															
ASSET	PATIENCE																															
LIABILITY	HATE																															
ASSET	LOVE																															
LIABILITY	RESENTMENT																															
ASSET	FORGIVENESS																															
LIABILITY	FALSE PRIDE																															
ASSET	SIMPLICITY																															
LIABILITY	JEALOUSY																															
ASSET	TRUST																															
LIABILITY	ENVY																															
ASSET	GENEROSITY																															
LIABILITY	LAZINESS																															
ASSET	ACTIVITY																															
LIABILITY	PROCRASTINATION																															
ASSET	PROMPTNESS																															
LIABILITY	INSINCERITY																															
ASSET	STRAIGHTFORWARDNESS																															
LIABILITY	NEGATIVE THINKING																															
ASSET	POSITIVE THINKING																															
LIABILITY	VULGAR, IMMORAL, TRASHY THINKING																															
ASSET	HIGH-MINDED, SPIRITUAL, CLEAN THINKING																															
LIABILITY	CRITICIZING																															
ASSET	LOOK FOR THE GOOD																															

*At the end of each month, review your chart and write a brief analysis using the worksheet on the following page.

The Little Red Book Study Guide. ©1998 by Hazelden Foundation. All rights reserved. Reproduction for personal use is permissible.

My Daily Inventory Review*

MONTH _____   YEAR _____

Instructions: At the end of each month, review your chart and write a brief analysis below.

1. Areas in which I improved:

_____

_____

_____

_____

_____

_____

2. Areas in need of improvement:

_____

_____

_____

_____

_____

_____

3. Other goals for next month:

_____

_____

_____

_____

_____

_____

The Little Red Book Study Guide. ©1998 by Hazelden Foundation. All rights reserved. Reproduction for personal use is permissible.

MY DAILY INVENTORY*   MONTH _____   YEAR _____

INSTRUCTIONS: At the end of each day, rate areas that you need to be aware of with an **X**, and put a ✔ next to areas in which you **made progress**.

		1	2	3	4	5	6	7	8	9	10	11	12	13	14	15	16	17	18	19	20	21	22	23	24	25	26	27	28	29	30	31
LIABILITY	SELF-PITY																															
ASSET	SELF-FORGETFULNESS																															
LIABILITY	SELF-JUSTIFICATION																															
ASSET	HUMILITY																															
LIABILITY	SELF-IMPORTANCE																															
ASSET	MODESTY																															
LIABILITY	SELF-CONDEMNATION																															
ASSET	SELF-VALUATION																															
LIABILITY	DISHONESTY																															
ASSET	HONESTY																															
LIABILITY	IMPATIENCE																															
ASSET	PATIENCE																															
LIABILITY	HATE																															
ASSET	LOVE																															
LIABILITY	RESENTMENT																															
ASSET	FORGIVENESS																															
LIABILITY	FALSE PRIDE																															
ASSET	SIMPLICITY																															
LIABILITY	JEALOUSY																															
ASSET	TRUST																															
LIABILITY	ENVY																															
ASSET	GENEROSITY																															
LIABILITY	LAZINESS																															
ASSET	ACTIVITY																															
LIABILITY	PROCRASTINATION																															
ASSET	PROMPTNESS																															
LIABILITY	INSINCERITY																															
ASSET	STRAIGHTFORWARDNESS																															
LIABILITY	NEGATIVE THINKING																															
ASSET	POSITIVE THINKING																															
LIABILITY	VULGAR, IMMORAL, TRASHY THINKING																															
ASSET	HIGH-MINDED, SPIRITUAL, CLEAN THINKING																															
LIABILITY	CRITICIZING																															
ASSET	LOOK FOR THE GOOD																															

*At the end of each month, review your chart and write a brief analysis using the worksheet on the following page.

The Little Red Book Study Guide. ©1998 by Hazelden Foundation. All rights reserved. Reproduction for personal use is permissible.

MY DAILY INVENTORY REVIEW*

INSTRUCTIONS: At the end of each month, review your chart and write a brief analysis below.

1. Areas in which I improved:

_____

_____

_____

_____

_____

2. Areas in need of improvement:

_____

_____

_____

_____

_____

3. Other goals for next month:

_____

_____

_____

_____

_____

The Little Red Book Study Guide. ©1998 by Hazelden Foundation. All rights reserved. Reproduction for personal use is permissible.

MY DAILY INVENTORY*

MONTH _____ YEAR _____

INSTRUCTIONS: At the end of each day, rate areas that you need to **beware of** with an **X**, and put a ✔ next to areas in which you **made progress.**

		1	2	3	4	5	6	7	8	9	10	11	12	13	14	15	16	17	18	19	20	21	22	23	24	25	26	27	28	29	30	31
LIABILITY	SELF-PITY																															
ASSET	SELF-FORGETFULNESS																															
LIABILITY	SELF-JUSTIFICATION																															
ASSET	HUMILITY																															
LIABILITY	SELF-IMPORTANCE																															
ASSET	MODESTY																															
LIABILITY	SELF-CONDEMNATION																															
ASSET	SELF-VALUATION																															
LIABILITY	DISHONESTY																															
ASSET	HONESTY																															
LIABILITY	IMPATIENCE																															
ASSET	PATIENCE																															
LIABILITY	HATE																															
ASSET	LOVE																															
LIABILITY	RESENTMENT																															
ASSET	FORGIVENESS																															
LIABILITY	FALSE PRIDE																															
ASSET	SIMPLICITY																															
LIABILITY	JEALOUSY																															
ASSET	TRUST																															
LIABILITY	ENVY																															
ASSET	GENEROSITY																															
LIABILITY	LAZINESS																															
ASSET	ACTIVITY																															
LIABILITY	PROCRASTINATION																															
ASSET	PROMPTNESS																															
LIABILITY	INSINCERITY																															
ASSET	STRAIGHTFORWARDNESS																															
LIABILITY	NEGATIVE THINKING																															
ASSET	POSITIVE THINKING																															
LIABILITY	VULGAR, IMMORAL, TRASHY THINKING																															
ASSET	HIGH-MINDED, SPIRITUAL, CLEAN THINKING																															
LIABILITY	CRITICIZING																															
ASSET	LOOK FOR THE GOOD																															

*At the end of each month, review your chart and write a brief analysis using the worksheet on the following page.

The Little Red Book Study Guide. ©1998 by Hazelden Foundation. All rights reserved. Reproduction for personal use is permissible.

MY DAILY INVENTORY REVIEW*

MONTH _____ YEAR _____

INSTRUCTIONS: At the end of each month, review your chart and write a brief analysis below.

1. Areas in which I improved:

_____
_____
_____
_____
_____

2. Areas in need of improvement:

_____
_____
_____
_____
_____

3. Other goals for next month:

_____
_____
_____
_____
_____

The Little Red Book Study Guide. ©1998 by Hazelden Foundation. All rights reserved. Reproduction for personal use is permissible.

MY DAILY INVENTORY* MONTH _____ YEAR _____

INSTRUCTIONS: At the end of each day, rate areas that you need to beware of with an X, and put a ✔ next to areas in which you made progress.

		1	2	3	4	5	6	7	8	9	10	11	12	13	14	15	16	17	18	19	20	21	22	23	24	25	26	27	28	29	30	31
LIABILITY	SELF-PITY																															
ASSET	SELF-FORGETFULNESS																															
LIABILITY	SELF-JUSTIFICATION																															
ASSET	HUMILITY																															
LIABILITY	SELF-IMPORTANCE																															
ASSET	MODESTY																															
LIABILITY	SELF-CONDEMNATION																															
ASSET	SELF-VALUATION																															
LIABILITY	DISHONESTY																															
ASSET	HONESTY																															
LIABILITY	IMPATIENCE																															
ASSET	PATIENCE																															
LIABILITY	HATE																															
ASSET	LOVE																															
LIABILITY	RESENTMENT																															
ASSET	FORGIVENESS																															
LIABILITY	FALSE PRIDE																															
ASSET	SIMPLICITY																															
LIABILITY	JEALOUSY																															
ASSET	TRUST																															
LIABILITY	ENVY																															
ASSET	GENEROSITY																															
LIABILITY	LAZINESS																															
ASSET	ACTIVITY																															
LIABILITY	PROCRASTINATION																															
ASSET	PROMPTNESS																															
LIABILITY	INSINCERITY																															
ASSET	STRAIGHTFORWARDNESS																															
LIABILITY	NEGATIVE THINKING																															
ASSET	POSITIVE THINKING																															
LIABILITY	VULGAR, IMMORAL, TRASHY THINKING																															
ASSET	HIGH-MINDED, SPIRITUAL, CLEAN THINKING																															
LIABILITY	CRITICIZING																															
ASSET	LOOK FOR THE GOOD																															

*At the end of each month, review your chart and write a brief analysis using the worksheet on the following page.

The Little Red Book Study Guide. ©1998 by Hazelden Foundation. All rights reserved. Reproduction for personal use is permissible.

MY DAILY INVENTORY REVIEW*

MONTH _____ YEAR _____

INSTRUCTIONS: At the end of each month, review your chart and write a brief analysis below.

1. Areas in which I improved:

_____

_____

_____

_____

_____

2. Areas in need of improvement:

_____

_____

_____

_____

_____

3. Other goals for next month:

_____

_____

_____

_____

_____

The *Little Red Book Study Guide.* ©1998 by Hazelden Foundation. All rights reserved. Reproduction for personal use is permissible.